CONTENTS

All songs written for the 1945 movie version of STATE FAIR unless otherwise noted.

4
Rodgers & Hammerstein Biography

6
Synopsis

8
History of the Show

10
All I Owe Ioway

19
Boys and Girls Like You and Me**

22
Isn't It Kinda Fun

27
It Might As Well Be Spring

32
It's a Grand Night for Singing

36
It's the Little Things in Texas*

40
The Man I Used to Be**

44
More Than Just a Friend*

48
Never Say "No"*

54
The Next Time It Happens**

66
Our State Fair

61
So Far**

68
That's for Me

72
That's the Way It Happens**

76
This Isn't Heaven*

79
When I Go Out Walking with My Baby**

82
Willing and Eager*

85
You Never Had It So Good**

**Written for the 1962 movie version, with lyrics by Richard Rodgers*
***Interpolated into the 1996 stage version*

Poster from STATE FAIR, Rodgers and Hammerstein's only musical written for Hollywood (1945 version)

RICHARD RODGERS & OSCAR HAMMERSTEIN II

After long and highly distinguished careers with other collaborators, Richard Rodgers (composer) and Oscar Hammerstein II (librettist/lyricist) joined forces to create the most consistently fruitful and successful partnership in the American musical theatre.

Prior to his work with Hammerstein, Richard Rodgers (1902-1979) collaborated with lyricist Lorenz Hart on a series of musical comedies that epitomized the wit and sophistication of Broadway in its heyday. Prolific on Broadway, in London and in Hollywood from the '20s into the early '40s, Rodgers & Hart wrote more than forty shows and film scores. Among their greatest were ON YOUR TOES, BABES IN ARMS, THE BOYS FROM SYRACUSE, I MARRIED AN ANGEL and PAL JOEY.

Throughout the same era Oscar Hammerstein II (1895-1960) brought new life to a moribund artform: the operetta. His collaborations with such preeminent composers as Rudolf Friml, Sigmund Romberg and Vincent Youmans resulted in such operetta classics as THE DESERT SONG, ROSE-MARIE and THE NEW MOON. With Jerome Kern he wrote SHOW BOAT, the 1927 masterpiece that changed the course of modern musical theatre. His last musical before embarking on an exclusive partnership with Richard Rodgers was CARMEN JONES, the highly-acclaimed 1943 all-black revision of Georges Bizet's tragic opera CARMEN.

OKLAHOMA!, the first Rodgers & Hammerstein musical, was also the first of a new genre, the musical play, representing a unique fusion of Rodgers' musical comedy and Hammerstein's operetta. A milestone in the development of the American musical, it also marked the beginning of the most successful partnership in Broadway musical history, and was followed by CAROUSEL, ALLEGRO, SOUTH PACIFIC, THE KING AND I, ME AND JULIET, PIPE DREAM, FLOWER DRUM SONG and THE SOUND OF MUSIC. Rodgers & Hammerstein wrote one musical specifically for the big screen, STATE FAIR, and one for television, CINDERELLA. Collectively, the Rodgers & Hammerstein musicals earned 35 Tony

United States postage stamp honoring Rodgers and Hammerstein, issued September 21, 1999.

SOMETHING GOOD
A Broadway Salute to Richard Rodgers on His 100th Birthday
Friday, June 28, 2002
Gershwin Theatre • New York City

Awards, 15 Academy Awards, two Pulitzer Prizes, two Grammy Awards and two Emmy Awards. In 1998 Rodgers & Hammerstein were cited by *Time* Magazine and CBS News as among the 20 most influential artists of the 20th century, and in 1999 they were jointly commemorated on a U.S. postage stamp.

Despite Hammerstein's death in 1960, Rodgers continued to write for the Broadway stage. His first solo entry, NO STRINGS, earned him two Tony Awards for music and lyrics, and was followed by DO I HEAR A WALTZ?, TWO BY TWO, REX and I REMEMBER MAMA. Richard Rodgers died on December 30, 1979, less than eight months after his last musical opened on Broadway. In March of 1990, Broadway's 46th Street Theatre was renamed The Richard Rodgers Theatre in his honor.

At the turn of the 21st century, the Rodgers and Hammerstein legacy continued to flourish, as marked by the enthusiasm that greeted their Centennials in 1995 and 2002.

In 1995, Hammerstein's centennial was celebrated worldwide with commemorative recordings, books, concerts and an award-winning PBS special, "Some Enchanted Evening." The ultimate tribute came the following season, when he had three musicals playing on Broadway simultaneously: SHOW BOAT (1995 Tony Award winner, Best Musical Revival); THE KING AND I (1996 Tony Award winner, Best Musical Revival); and STATE FAIR (1996 Tony Award nominee for Best Score).

In 2002, the Richard Rodgers Centennial was celebrated around the world, with tributes from Tokyo to London, from the Hollywood Bowl to the White House, featuring six new television specials, museum retrospectives, a dozen new ballets, half a dozen books, new recordings and countless concert and stage productions (including three simultaneous revivals on Broadway, matching Hammerstein's feat of six years earlier), giving testament to the enduring popularity of Richard Rodgers and the sound of his music.

SYNOPSIS OF THE STAGE MUSICAL

ACT ONE

It is late summer in 1946 on the Frake family farm in Brunswick, Iowa. The Frakes are preparing to leave for the Iowa State Fair (**"Our State Fair"**). Father Abel is confident his prize boar, Blue Boy, will win a blue ribbon, but neighbor Dave Miller isn't so sure. He makes a five-dollar bet that something is bound to go wrong for a least one member of the family. Abel accepts the bet.

Abel's wife, Melissa, has her heart set on a blue ribbon for her mincemeat. Son Wayne is disappointed that his girlfriend has to stay home. Daughter Margy is feeling down and doesn't understand why. (**"It Might As Well Be Spring"**). Her suitor, Harry, pressures her for an answer to his long-standing marriage proposal; she agrees to give him an answer when she returns home.

Newspaper reporter Pat Gilbert (Dana Andrews) shows farmgirl Margy Frake (Jeanne Crain) the wonders of the midway in STATE FAIR (1945).

"Isn't It Kinda Fun": Andrea McArdle and Scott Wise in the 1996 Broadway production of STATE FAIR
Photo © Carol Rosegg

Donna McKechnie as the showgirl Emily, flanked by Ian Knauer and Michael Lee Scott, from the 1996 Broadway production of STATE FAIR.
Photo © Carol Rosegg

So it's off to the Fair. Arriving at the midway, Wayne heads straight for the ring toss where he is hustled by the barker. A glamorous woman intercedes on Wayne's behalf. He is smitten before he even gets to know who she is (**"That's for Me"**). At the beer tent, Abel and his cronies sit around telling stories about their loved ones (**"More Than Just a Friend"**). Meanwhile, a young and somewhat world-weary reporter, Pat Gilbert, arrives to cover the Fair. He sets his sights on Margy, who remains aloof until he begins to win her over (**"Isn't It Kinda Fun"**).

Wayne happens by the Starlight Dance Meadow in time to catch the floor show. The star attraction is Emily Arden, the woman he met earlier in the day (**"You Never Had It So Good"**). Over a beer, she tells Wayne she is determined to become a Broadway star. He asks for a date, charming her with his boyish enthusiasm. She agrees, but on her terms: "nothing complicated, always leave 'em laughing."

The next morning, Margy bemoans the life Harry is planning for them. Abel is so excited at the prospect of victory and winning his bet with Dave Miller that he proposes an evening of family fun and dancing (**"When I Go Out Walking with My Baby"**).

At the Exhibit Hall that afternoon the pickles and mincemeat are being judged. As it happens, Melissa's mincemeat has been amply spiked, which sends the judges into giggles of delight. She wins the blue ribbon *and* a special plaque. Pat is on hand to capture the euphoric moment.

From a moonlit hill, Wayne and Emily watch the Fair below. He has fallen head over heels, but she remains cautious (**"So Far"**). At the Starlight Dance Meadow, fairgoers gather for a dreamy waltz (**"It's a Grand Night for Singing"**). Abel and Melissa dance romantically. Wayne and Emily arrive with a distinct glow, and Pat and Margy share a first tentative kiss as Harry arrives unexpectedly. "I'll bet you're surprised to see me," he asks a stunned Margy. "You have no idea," she replies as the curtain falls.

REVISED EDITION

STATE FAIR

Music by
Richard Rodgers

Lyrics by
Oscar Hammerstein II

Cover Photo © Carol Rosegg

ISBN 0-88188-116-3

WILLIAMSON MUSIC®
A RODGERS AND HAMMERSTEIN COMPANY
www.williamsonmusic.com

EXCLUSIVELY DISTRIBUTED BY

7777 W. BLUEMOUND RD. P.O. BOX 13819 MILWAUKEE, WI 53213

Visit Hal Leonard Online at
www.halleonard.com

Rodgers and Hammerstein's

"PERFECTION!... JUST PIN THAT BLUE RIBBON ON THE THEATER MARQUEE!"

— Chicago Sun-Times

To learn more about STATE FAIR and the other great musicals available for production through The Rodgers & Hammerstein Theatre Library, please visit our award-winning website **www.rnh.com** or contact

229 W. 28TH ST., 11th FLOOR
NEW YORK, NEW YORK 10001

PHONE: (212)564-4000
FAX: (212)268-1245
E-MAIL: theatre@rnh.com

The offering of this publication for sale is not to be construed as authorization for the performance of any material contained herein. Applications for the right to perform STATE FAIR, in whole or in part, should be addressed to The Rodgers & Hammerstein Theatre Library.

NOTE: Not all of the songs featured in this songbook appear in the authorized stage version.

All photos (unless otherwise noted) provided courtesy of The Rodgers & Hammerstein Organization

Copyright © 2004 by WILLIAMSON MUSIC
International Copyright Secured All Rights Reserved

Rodgers and Hammerstein is a trademark of the Family Trust u/w Richard Rodgers, the Family Trust u/w Dorothy F. Rodgers and the Estate of Oscar Hammerstein II.

The R&H logo and Williamson Music are registered trademarks of the Family Trust u/w Richard Rodgers, the Family Trust u/w Dorothy F. Rodgers and the Estate of Oscar Hammerstein II.

For all works contained herein:
Unauthorized copying, arranging, adapting, recording or public performance is an infringement of copyright.
Infringers are liable under the law.

Pat Boone as Wayne, and Ann-Margret as Emily in the 1962 movie remake of STATE FAIR.

Jeanne Crain as Margy Frake, and Dana Andrews as newspaper reporter Pat Gilbert in the original 1945 movie musical version of STATE FAIR.

ACT TWO

It is the final day of the Fair. Despite Harry's presence, Pat and Margy are clearly growing fond of each other. As Margy rushes off to cheer for Blue Boy, Pat's friends help him realize he is no longer his old self (**"The Man I Used to Be"**). Blue Boy is finally declared the winner of the hog-judging competition, and Abel cannot contain his joy. "Nothin' fine as Ioway swine," he crows, and everyone agrees (**"All I Owe Ioway"**).

Pat learns he has secured the Chicago job interview he has been waiting for, but it means catching the next train out of town. Reluctant to leave Margy in the lurch, he races off just as she arrives for their date.
The scene shifts to the Starlight Dance Meadow and Emily Arden's final performance. Both women realize their relationships are in trouble (**"That's the Way It Happens"**).

Abel Frake (John Davidson) and his wife Melissa Frake (Kathryn Crosby) in the 1996 Broadway production of STATE FAIR.
Photo © Carol Rosegg

Later that night, Wayne proclaims his love for Emily, but she breaks it off. Back at the family campsite, Abel and Melissa are basking in their victories. Melissa is concerned about the children, but Abel assures her that they have each other (**"Boys and Girls Like You and Me"**). Wayne staggers in, having drowned his sorrows. In his stupor, however, his thoughts turn to his girl back home. Understandingly, Abel helps his son "walk it off."

The Frake family reads all about their exploits at the Iowa State Fair—John Davidson, Ben Wright, Kathryn Crosby and Andrea McArdle from the 1996 Broadway production of STATE FAIR.
Photo © Carol Rosegg

On the darkened midway Margy is still waiting for Pat. The fair is almost over, and she realizes he is probably not coming (**"The Next Time It Happens"**). Harry enters, pleading to Margy to accept his proposal. She can't—she realizes she just doesn't love him.

The Frakes return home. There is a spread in the local newspaper chronicling their adventures at the Fair—written, of course, by Pat Gilbert without any of them knowing. "Wait 'til Dave Miller reads this!" boasts Abel, but Dave reminds him that the bet hinged on *everyone* having a good time at the Fair. Wayne is thrilled to be home and is making big plans with his girlfriend, but Margy seems a little low. "Maybe I've outgrown the Fair," she says. And who should arrive that moment, but Pat. He's breathless and full of apologies—but he has landed the job in Chicago and wants Margy to join him there. The lovers rush into each other's arms as Miller reluctantly hands over the five dollars.

John Davidson as Abel Frake leads his fellow Iowans in "All I Owe Ioway" from the 1996 Broadway production of STATE FAIR.
Photo © Carol Rosegg

STATE FAIR – 50 YEARS FROM SCREEN TO STAGE

By Tom Briggs

The seventeen-year collaboration of composer Richard Rodgers and librettist Oscar Hammerstein II resulted in nine Broadway musicals. They are lead by the "Big Five"—OKLAHOMA! (1943), CAROUSEL (1945), SOUTH PACIFIC (1949), THE KING AND I (1951) and THE SOUND OF MUSIC (1959)—and also include ALLEGRO (1947), ME AND JULIET (1953), PIPE DREAM (1955) and FLOWER DRUM SONG (1958, revised 2002). They wrote one musical for television, CINDERELLA (1957, remade in 1965 and 1997), and one musical expressly for the big screen, STATE FAIR (1945, remade in 1962). CINDERELLA had been successfully adapted for the stage, and so it was that STATE FAIR remained the only Rodgers and Hammerstein musical without a life on the stage.

Phil Stong's novel *State Fair* was published in 1932 and a non-musical motion picture version was released the following year starring Will Rogers, Janet Gaynor and Lew Ayres. Twelve years later, fresh on the heels of their triumph with OKLAHOMA!, Rodgers & Hammerstein's STATE FAIR came to the screen starring Charles Winninger, Fay Bainter, Jeanne Crain, Dick Haymes, Dana Andrews and Vivian Blaine, winning R&H the Academy Award for their song, "It Might As Well Be Spring." A 1962 remake updated the story and transplanted it from its original Iowa setting to Texas. It followed the death of Hammerstein by two years, so Rodgers augmented the score with songs for which he wrote both the music and lyrics. It was with these combined resources—a novel and three movies—that my late collaborator, Louis Mattioli and I began our work in bringing STATE FAIR to the stage.

We were facing two major challenges. The first was the story, which, along with the characters and relationships, would clearly require deeper exploration and development for the stage. The second challenge was the score, for R&H wrote only six songs for the 1945 picture, and six songs do not a theatrical score make. We clearly needed to include other songs which would have to blend stylistically with those from the movies, illuminate the various characters and situations and, above all (as R&H taught us), propel the story forward. And of course the songs could not be indelibly associated with other R&H musicals—we would not be interpolating "Climb Ev'ry Mountain" or "Some Enchanted Evening."

Original sheet music cover

Unlike many writers, R&H did not leave behind a plethora of undiscovered songs, known in show-biz parlance as "trunk material." Seldom was a song they wrote replaced in a show and when it was, it often found a home in a subsequent musical. ("Getting to Know You" from THE KING AND I began life as the melody of "Suddenly Lovely" written for SOUTH PACIFIC. "Younger Than Springtime" from SOUTH PACIFIC was originally written as "My Wife" for ALLEGRO.) And R&H were theatre writers who rarely wrote outside the context of the musicals they created so, all told, we realized that this extant material would not so much warrant a trunk as perhaps a knapsack.

We began our musical search with OKLAHOMA! I was familiar with a lovely song that had been cut out-of-town when the show was still called AWAY WE GO! It was just right for the parents of our young protagonists and so "Boys and Girls Like You and Me" became the seventh song in our STATE FAIR. We also discovered one of the earliest songs written for OKLAHOMA! which had never even made it into rehearsal—a snappy cakewalk entitled "When I Go Out Walking with My Baby."

Because we were setting the show in the postwar '40s, we wanted the score to resonate with the Big Band sound of that era. Now swing music is not the first thing you associate with the names Rodgers and Hammerstein, and yet we felt it might be a welcome stylistic surprise. And because one of the characters is a band singer, it was opportune to incorporate some musical arrangements that jumped a bit more than might be expected from R&H. Two songs written for ME AND JULIET fit the bill perfectly—"You Never Had It So Good" (cut prior to Broadway) and "That's the Way It Happens."

We rounded out the score with "The Man I Used to Be" and "The Next Time It Happens" from PIPE DREAM, "So Far" from ALLEGRO, and "More Than Just a Friend" from the 1962 remake of STATE FAIR. Fourteen songs in all—now that's a theatrical score!

It took fifty years for STATE FAIR to take its rightful place as the eleventh stage musical borne out of the extraordinary partnership of Rodgers and Hammerstein, and it was worth the wait. Now every R&H score can be experienced in the environment they clearly loved best—the live theater.

Presented by David Merrick, the stage version of STATE FAIR opened on Broadway on March 27, 1996, starring John Davidson, Kathryn Crosby, Andrea McArdle and Donna McKechnie. With music by Richard Rodgers, lyrics by Oscar Hammerstein II , a book by Tom Briggs and Louis Mattioli based on the screenplay by Oscar Hammerstein II and the novel by Phil Stong, it was choreographed by Randy Skinner, and co-directed by James Hammerstein and Randy Skinner.

A scene from the 1996 Broadway production of STATE FAIR.
Photo © Carol Rosegg

ALL I OWE IOWAY

Lyrics by OSCAR HAMMERSTEIN II
Music by RICHARD RODGERS

Copyright © 1945 by WILLIAMSON MUSIC
Copyright Renewed
International Copyright Secured All Rights Reserved

G6
G
D
I - ow - ay in your heart! Leader: I've got I - ow - ay in my
A
Bm
E7
hair, I've got I - ow - ay in my ears and eyes and
A
Em7
A
Refrain
D
Dmaj7
nose. Leader: Oh I know all I
know all I
know all I
mf
D6
D+
D
owe, I owe I - ow - ay, I owe
owe, I owe I - ow - ay, I owe
owe, I owe I - ow - ay, I owe

D6
Adim7
Em
Em+/A
I - ow - ay all I owe and I know why.
I - ow - ay all I owe and I know why.
I - ow - ay all I owe and I know why.

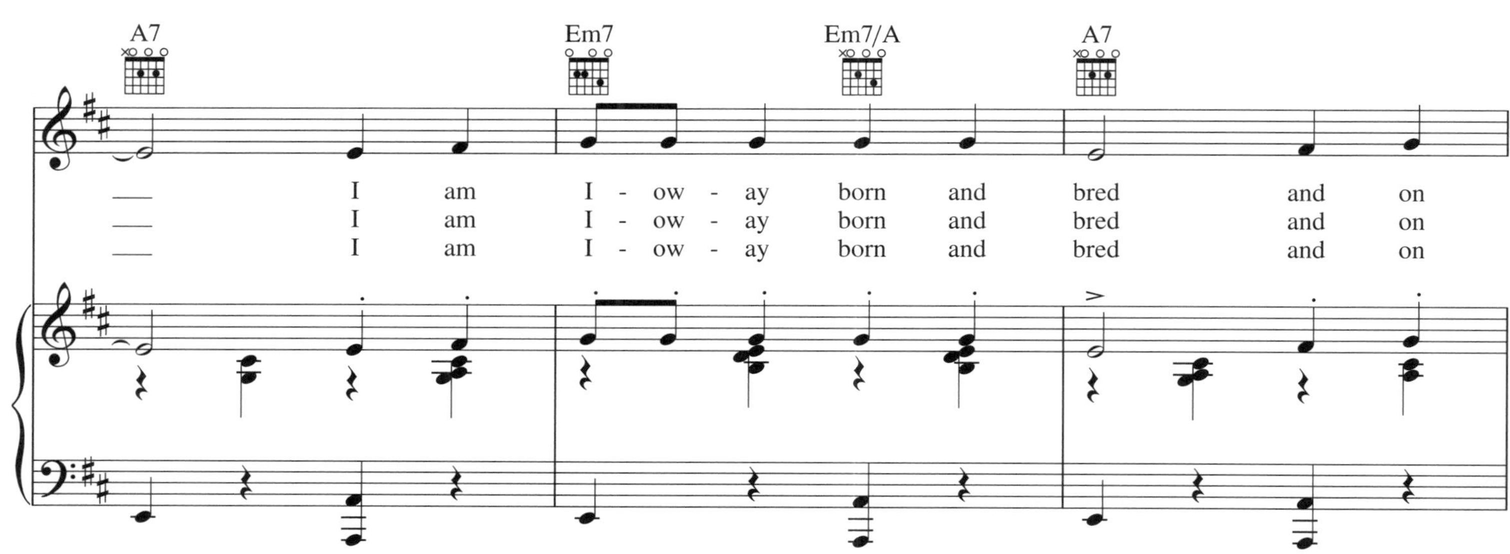
A7
Em7
Em7/A
A7
I am I - ow - ay born and bred and on
I am I - ow - ay born and bred and on
I am I - ow - ay born and bred and on

Dmaj7
D6
A
I - ow - ay corn I'm fed, not to men - tion her
I - ow - ay corn I'm fed, not to men - tion her
I - ow - ay corn I'm fed, not to men - tion her

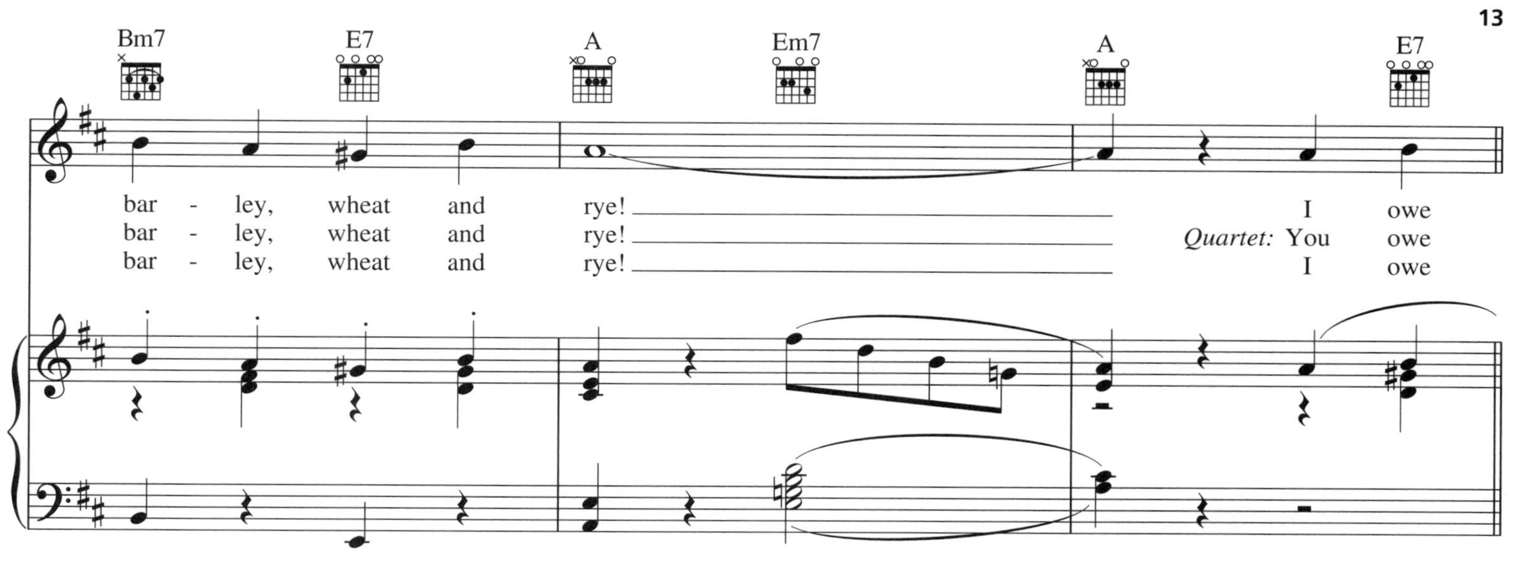
Bm7
E7
A
Em7
A
E7
bar - ley, wheat and rye!
bar - ley, wheat and rye!
bar - ley, wheat and rye!
I owe
Quartet: You owe
I owe

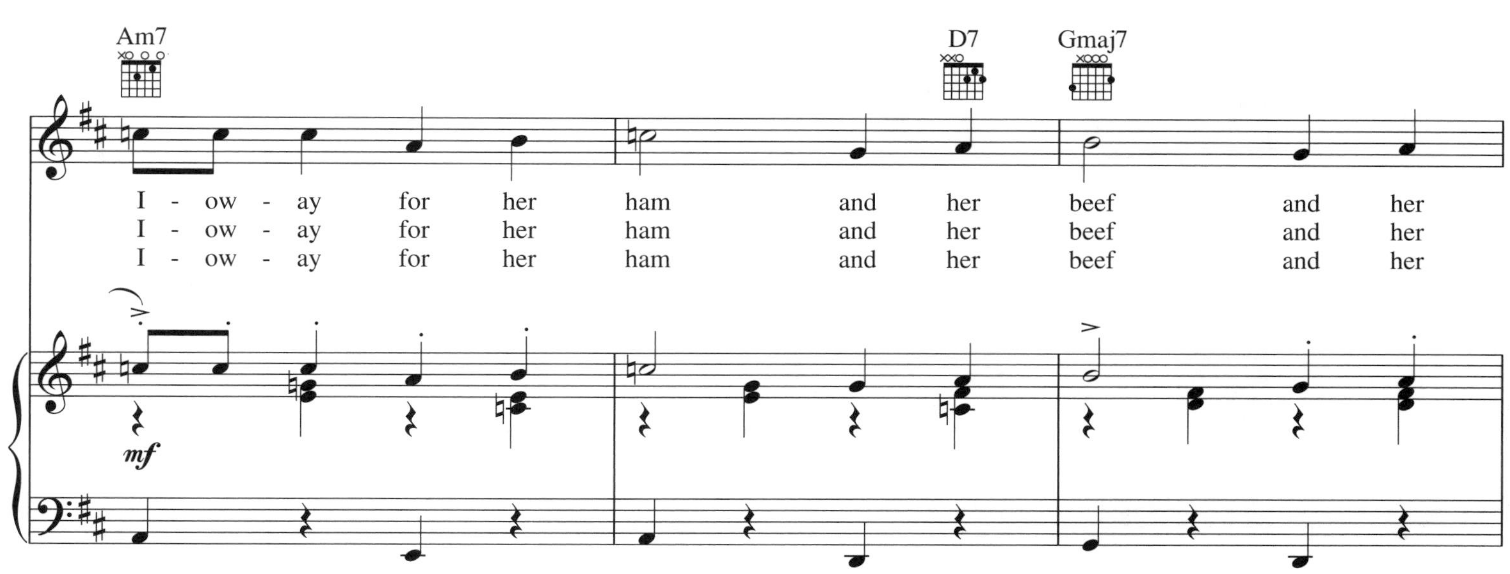
Am7
D7
Gmaj7
I - ow - ay for her ham and her beef and her
I - ow - ay for her ham and her beef and her
I - ow - ay for her ham and her beef and her
mf

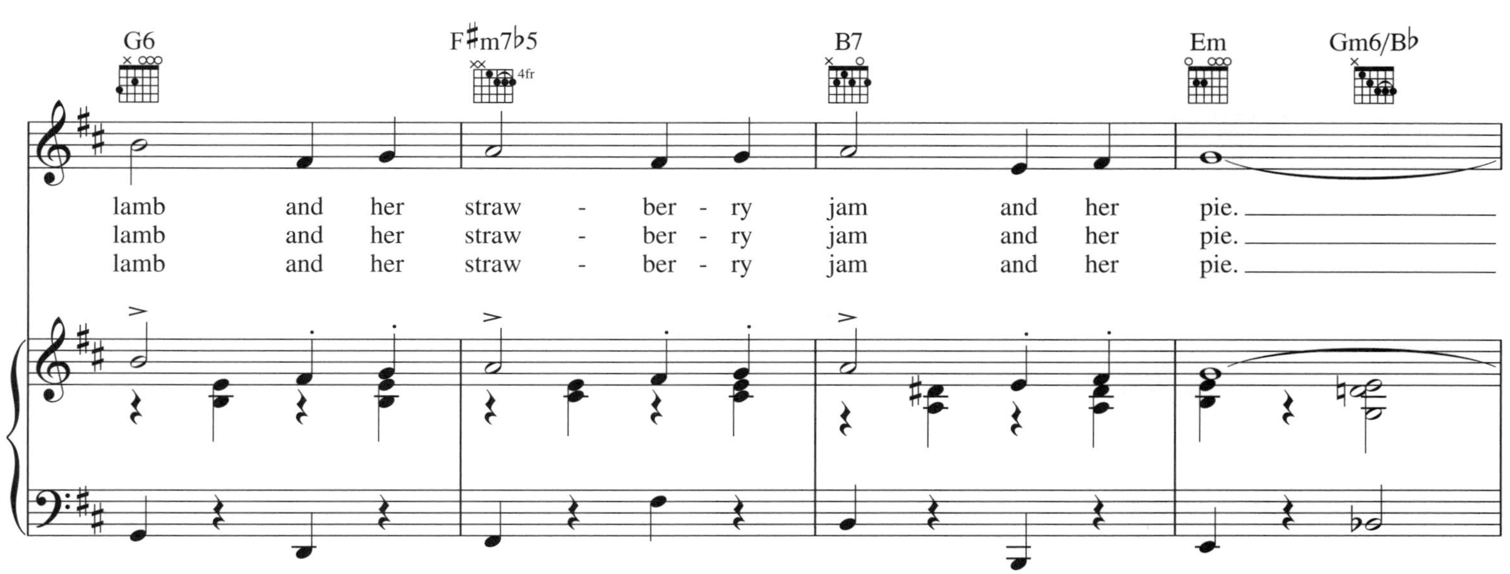
G6
F♯m7♭5
4fr
B7
Em
Gm6/B♭
lamb and her straw - ber - ry jam and her pie.
lamb and her straw - ber - ry jam and her pie.
lamb and her straw - ber - ry jam and her pie.

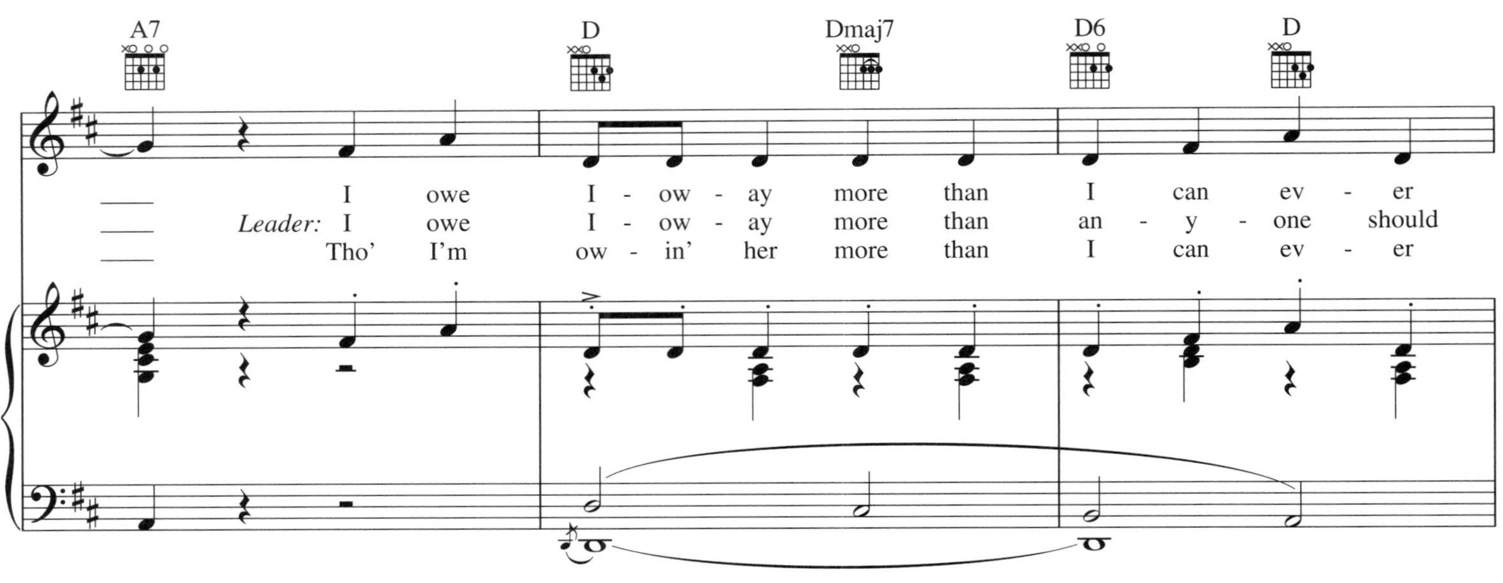
A7
D
Dmaj7
D6
D
I owe I - ow - ay more than I can ev - er
Leader: I owe I - ow - ay more than an - y - one should
Tho' I'm ow - in' her more than I can ev - er

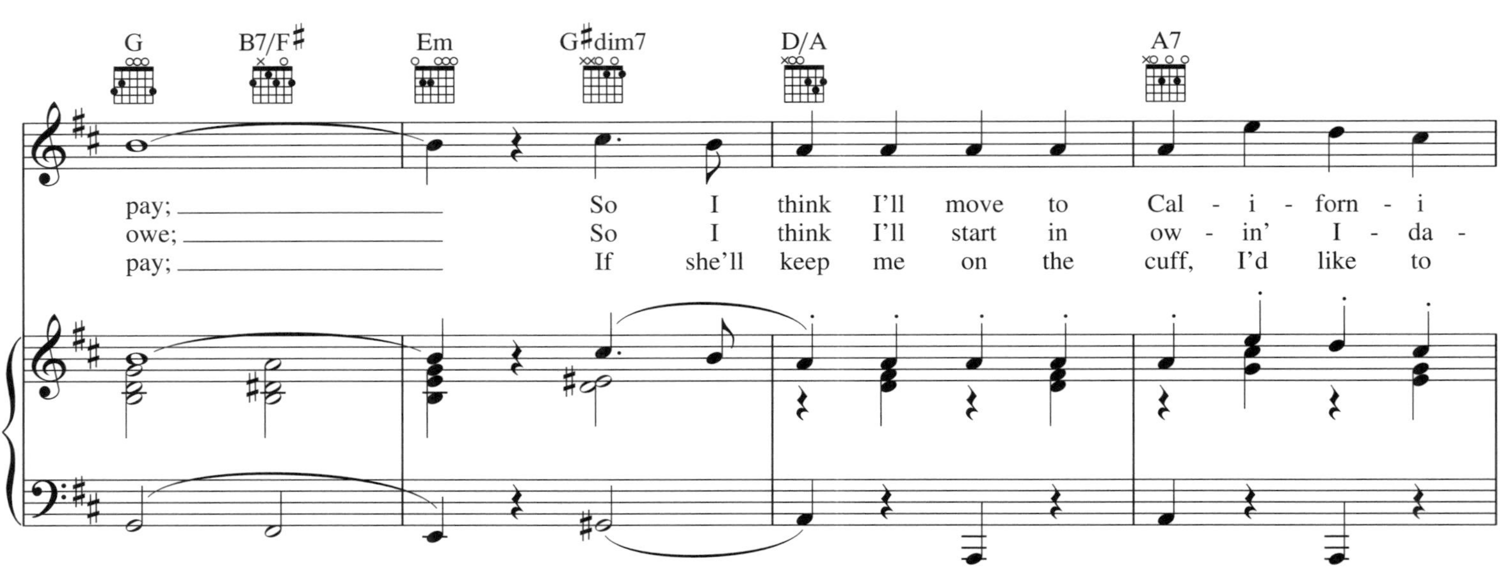
G
B7/F♯
Em
G♯dim7
D/A
A7
pay; So I think I'll move to Cal - i - forn - i
owe; So I think I'll start in ow - in' I - da -
pay; If she'll keep me on the cuff, I'd like to

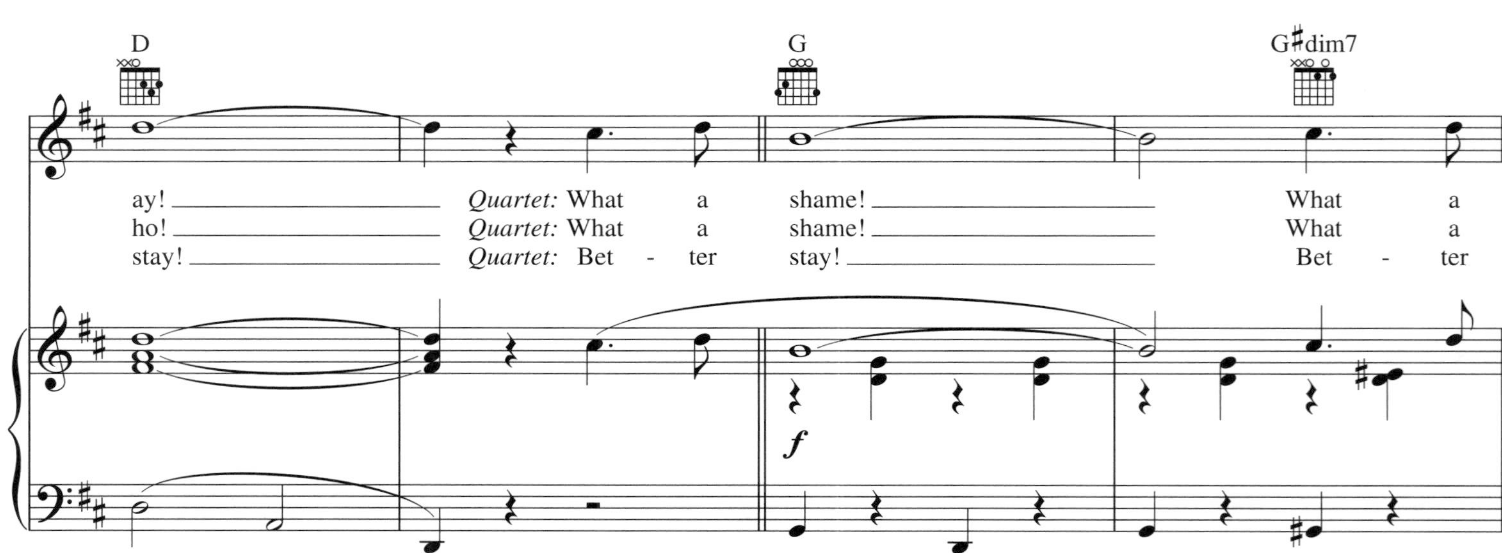
D
G
G♯dim7
ay! Quartet: What a shame! What a
ho! Quartet: What a shame! What a
stay! Quartet: Bet - ter stay! Bet - ter

D
Bm
Bm7
shame! You'll be good and gosh darn
shame! You'll be cry - in' like a
stay! You'll be good and gosh darn

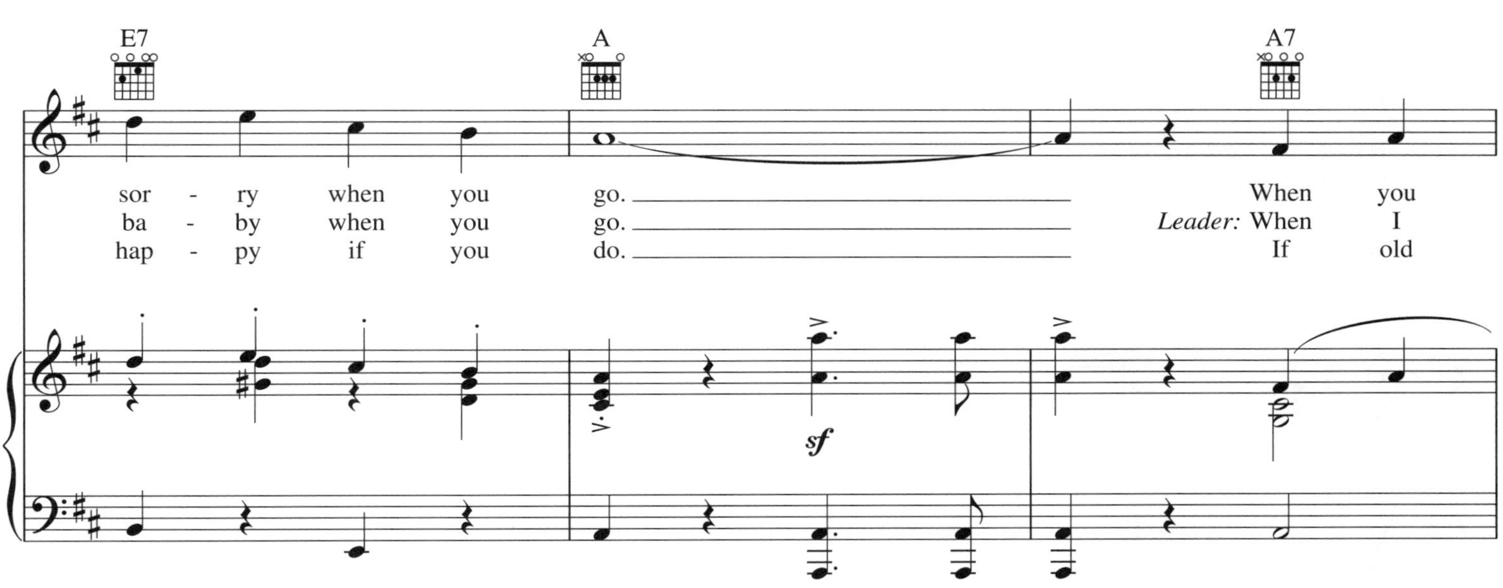
E7
A
A7
sor - ry when you go. When you
ba - by when you go. Leader: When I
hap - py if you do. If old
sf

D
Dmaj7
D6
D
G
B7/F#
leave your na - tive state, You'll be feel - in' far from
leave my na - tive heath With my lips be - tween my
I - ow - ay is your home You're a fool to want to

Em
G#dim7
D/A
A7
3rd time to Coda
great, You'll be good and gosh darn sor - ry when you
teeth, I'll be bawl - in' like a ba - by when I
roam, 'Cause there can't be an - y bet - ter home for

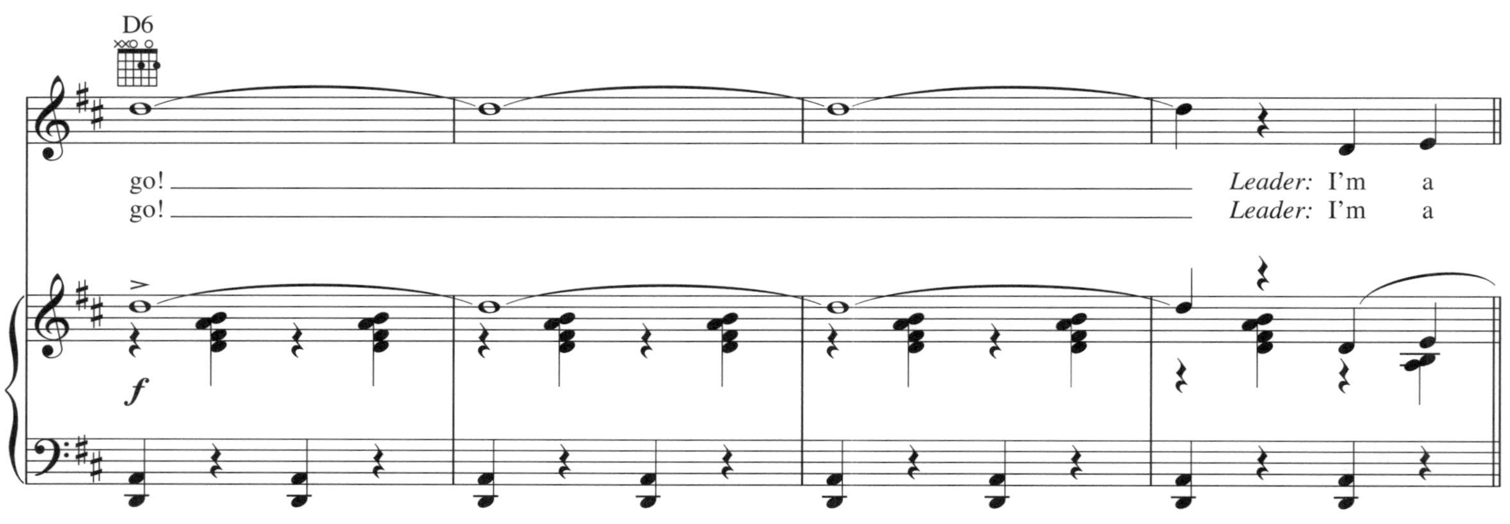
D6
go!
go!
Leader: I'm a
Leader: I'm a
f

D6
A9/D
5fr
seed of I - ow - ay grain
seed of I - ow - ay grain

Quartet: You're a breeze that I - ow - ay
Quartet: You're a breeze that I - ow - ay
D6
blew.
blew.
A6
Leader: I'm a drop
Leader: I'm a drop
E9/A
6fr
of I - ow - ay rain.
of I - ow - ay rain.
Quartet: You're a
Quartet: You're a
A
Adim7
drip of I - ow - ay dew!
drip of I - ow - ay dew!

A7

1st time D.S.
2nd time D.S. al Coda

Leader: Oh, I
Leader: Oh, I

CODA

D N.C. A7

you. If old

mf

D Dmaj7 D6 D G B7/F♯

I - ow - ay is your home, You're a fool to want to

cresc.

Em G♯dim7 D/A A7

roam, 'Cause there can't be an - y bet - ter home for

D6 D A7 D

you!

f *ff* *sf*

BOYS AND GIRLS LIKE YOU AND ME

Lyrics by OSCAR HAMMERSTEIN II
Music by RICHARD RODGERS

Copyright © 1943 by WILLIAMSON MUSIC
Copyright Renewed
International Copyright Secured All Rights Reserved

C7
Fm
C7
Fm
B♭m6
6fr
go through storms of doubt and fear, And so we walk from year to year, Be -
Fm
C7
Fm
liev - ing in each oth - er, as we do,
C/G
C+/G
Fmaj7/G
G9
9fr
C
C7
Brave - ly march - ing for - ward, two by two.
poco rit.
Refrain (slowly and with tenderness)
F6
F
Gm7
Boys and girls like you and me Walk be - neath the
3
p - mf

C7
F6
C7
F/A
C7
F
Fm6
skies. They love just as we love, With the same dream in their
poco a poco cresc.
C
C7
Cm7/F
8fr
F7
Cm7
3fr
F7
eyes. Songs and kings and man - y things
mf
B♭
Gm7♭5
F
G7
have their day and are gone, But boys and girls like you and me,
più espr.
C7
1
F
C9
2
F
We go on and on. on.
mf poco rit.
a tempo
f
Ped.
*

ISN'T IT KINDA FUN

Lyrics by OSCAR HAMMERSTEIN II
Music by RICHARD RODGERS

Copyright © 1945 by WILLIAMSON MUSIC
Copyright Renewed
International Copyright Secured All Rights Reserved

C
B7♯5
B7
She: I don't say our hearts are tied by love's e - ter - nal
Em
A7♯5
A7
F
Fm
teth - er, He: But us - ing words less dig - ni - fied,
G
C♯dim7
G7
Refrain
C
Dm7/G
Is - n't it kind - a fun to be to - geth - er? He: May - be you'll nev - er be the
f
mf - f
C
G7
C6
C9
love of my life, May - be I'm not the boy of your dreams, But

F
Fdim7
C/E
Am
3
is - n't it kind - a fun to look in each oth - er's eyes
Dm7
G9
9fr
G7♯5(♭9)
C
Dm7/G
Swap - ping ro - man - tic gleams?
May - be you're not a girl to
f
mf
C
G7
C6
C9
have and to hold,
May - be I'm not a boy who would stay,
But
F
Fdim7
C/E
Am
is - n't it kind - a fun ca - rous - ing a - round the town,

Dm7 G7 C Ab Ab+ Ab6
Danc - ing the nights a - way? Is - n't it kind - a fun hold - ing
più espr.
Ab7 C G7 F/C C
hands Ac - cord - ing to a sweet and corn - y cus - tom?
f
Ab Ab+ Ab6 Ab7
Is - n't it kind - a fun mak - ing vows ad -
mf
C G7 E7 A7 D9 G7 C Dm7/G
mit - ting that we both in - tend to bust 'em! May - be we're out for laughs, a
mp

C G7 C6 C9

girl and a boy, Kid - ding a - cross a ta - ble for two, But

F Fdim7 C/E Am

have - n't you got a hunch That this is the real Mc Coy, And

Dm7 F/G G7 1 C Am

all the things we tell each oth - er are true?

Dm G7 2 C Fdim7 C

true? ___

IT MIGHT AS WELL BE SPRING

Lyrics by OSCAR HAMMERSTEIN II
Music by RICHARD RODGERS

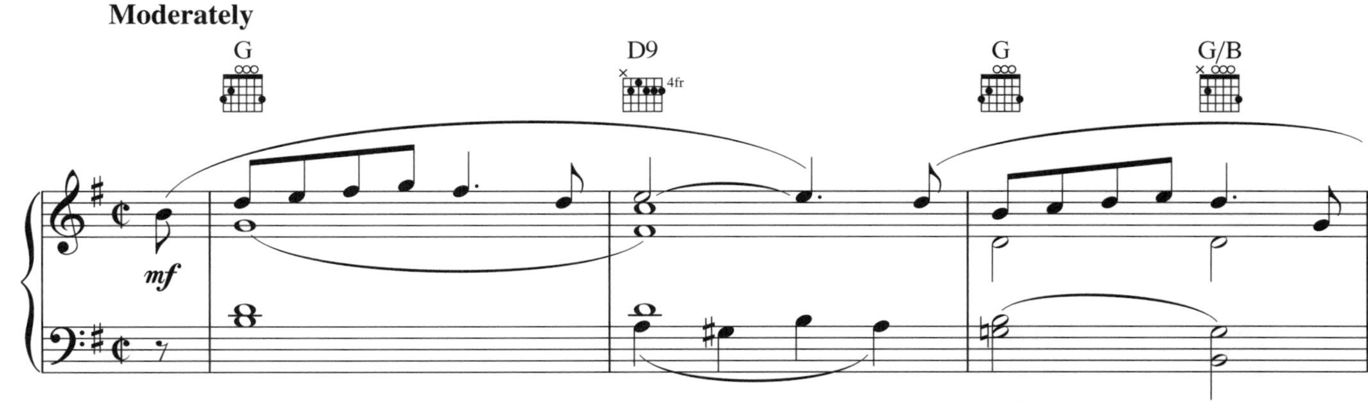

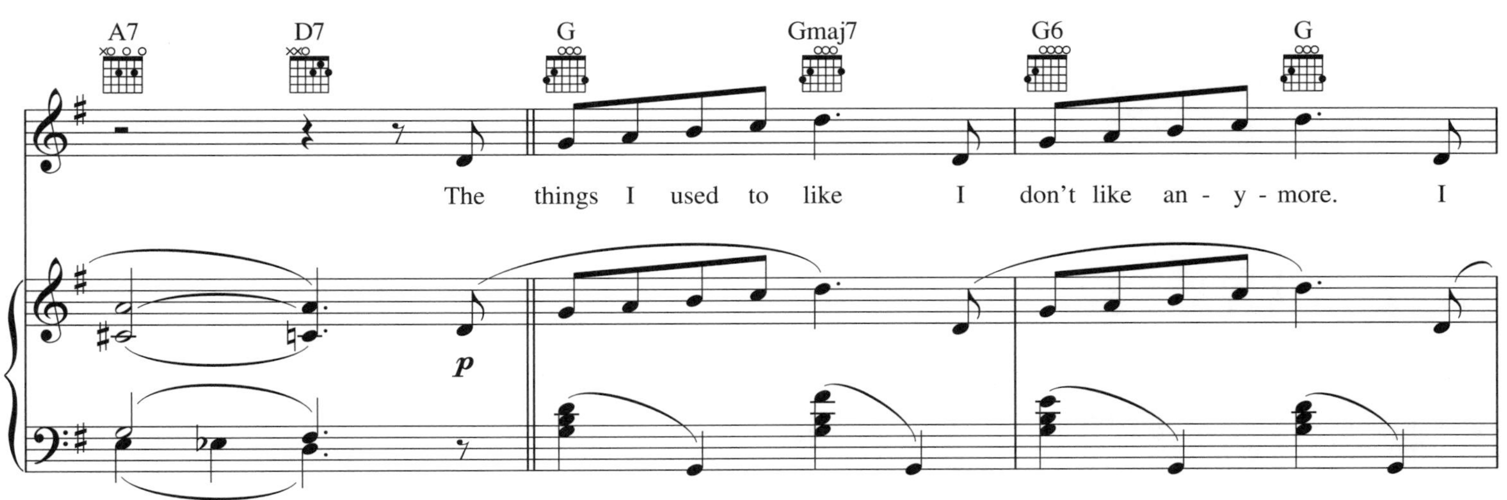

Copyright © 1945 by WILLIAMSON MUSIC
Copyright Renewed
International Copyright Secured All Rights Reserved

G/D
Am7
D7
G6
G
says, I "sit a - round and mope" Pre -
C
Am7♭5
G/D
Am7
D7
tend - ing I am won - der - ful and know - ing I'm a
G6
G
G6
G
Refrain (gracefully)
G
Gmaj7
dope.
I'm as rest - less as a wil - low in a
p - mf
G
Gmaj7
Dm7
G7
wind - storm, I'm as jump - y as a pup - pet on a string. I'd

C
Cdim7
G/B
G/D
Am7
D7
say that I had spring fe - ver, But I know it is - n't
Gmaj7
G6
G
Gmaj7
G
spring. I am star - ry - eyed and vague - ly dis - con - tent - ed, Like a
Gmaj7
Dm7
G7
C
Cdim7
night - in - gale with - out a song to sing. Oh, why should I have spring
G/B
G/D
Am7
D7
G
C
fe - ver When it is - n't e - ven spring? I keep wish - ing I were

Dm7 Dm7/G Dm7 G7♭5(♯9) G7 C

some - where else, walk - ing down a strange new street,

F♯m7 B7 Em/G A7 G D7 G D7

Hear - ing words that I have nev - er heard from a {man / girl} I've yet to meet. I'm as

cresc. *mf* *p*

G Gmaj7 G Gmaj7

bus - y as a spi - der spin - ning day - dreams, I'm as gid - dy as a ba - by on a

Dm7 G7 C Cdim7 G/B G/D

swing. I have - n't seen a cro - cus or a rose - bud, or a

C6
D9
4fr
B7
E7♭9
A7
rob - in on the wing,
But I feel so gay in a
D9
4fr
G7
A7
mel - an - cho - ly way that it might as well be spring.
It
G/D
D7sus
D7
1
G
Em
might as well be spring!
C
D7
2
G
C6
G
I'm as spring!
mf
mf

IT'S A GRAND NIGHT FOR SINGING

Lyrics by OSCAR HAMMERSTEIN II
Music by RICHARD RODGERS

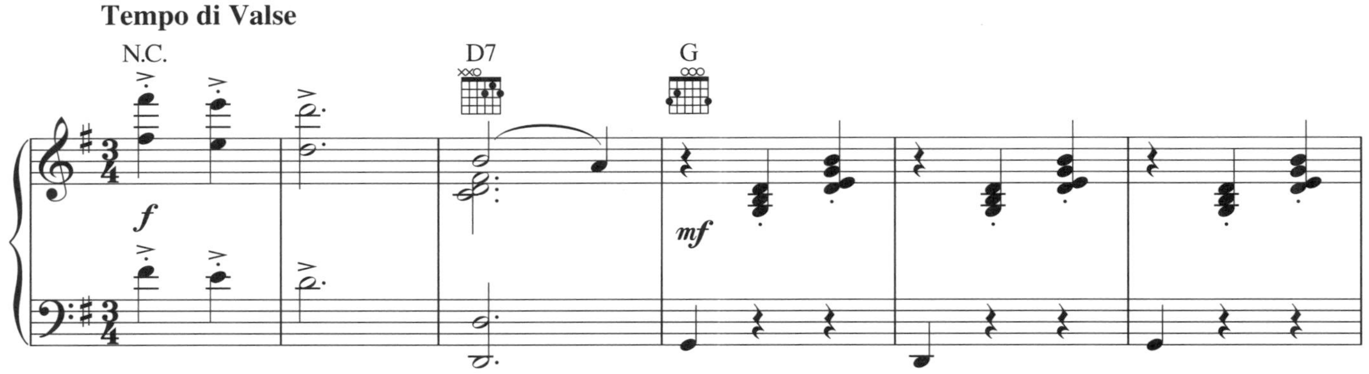

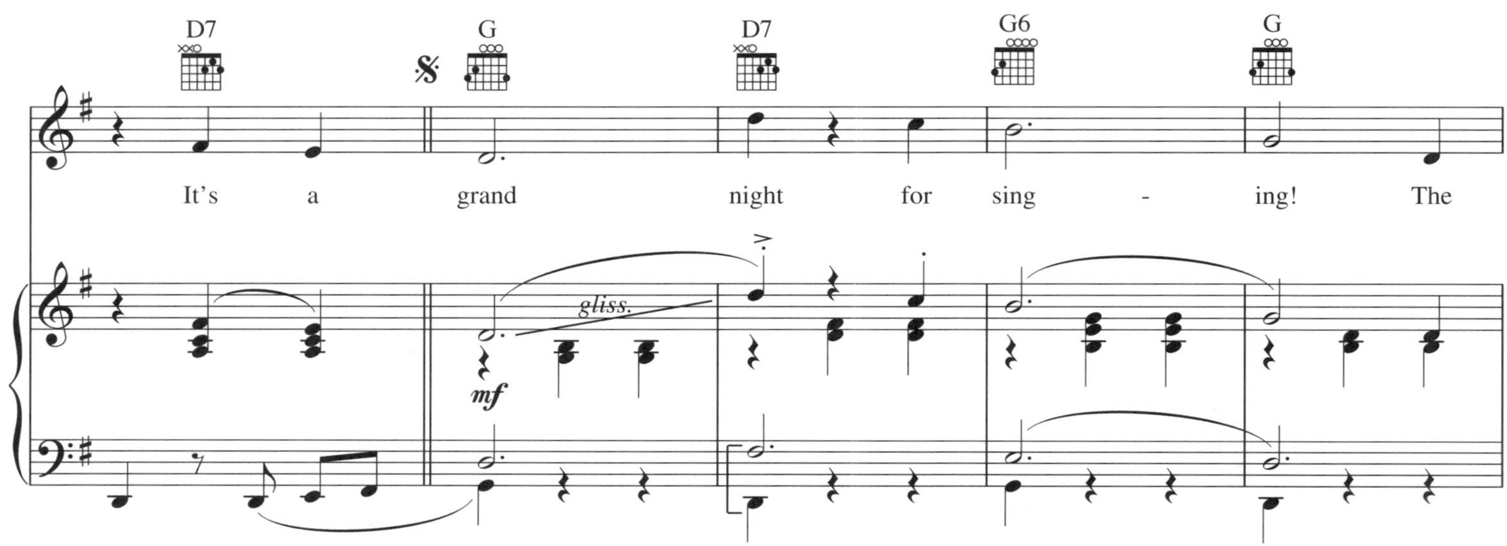

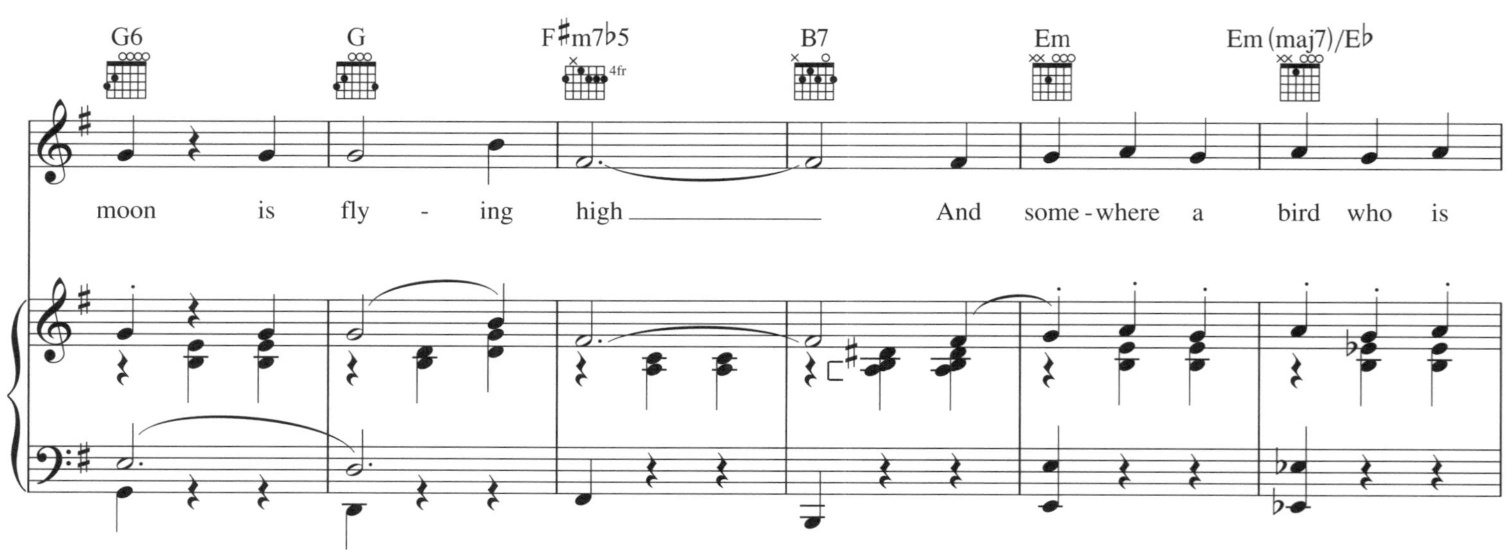

Copyright © 1945 by WILLIAMSON MUSIC
Copyright Renewed
International Copyright Secured All Rights Reserved

Em/D A7/C♯ Am7 D6 Gmaj7
bound he'll be heard, Is throw - ing his heart at the sky.
G6 D7 G D7 G6 G
It's a grand night for sing - ing! The
gliss.
G6 G F♯m7♭5 B7 Em
4fr
stars are bright a - bove, The earth is a -
Em(maj7)/E♭ Em/D A7/C♯ D7 G9
glow and to add to the show, I think I am fall - ing in

C7
G6/D
3fr
Am7
love.
Fall - ing,
Fall -
gliss.
gliss.
mf
D7
G
C6
G
Fine
ing in love.
mf
Interlude
N.C.
G
May - be it's more than the
mf
p
D9
4fr
D+
Gmaj7
moon,
May - be it's more than the birds.

B+ C A7/C♯ G/D A7/C♯
May - be it's more than the sight of the night in a light too love - ly for
Am7/D D7 G Am7 D7
words. May - be it's more than the earth
B C♯m7 F♯7 D/A
4fr
Shin - y and sil - ver - y blue. May - be the rea - son I'm
poco a poco cresc.
Adim7 Em7 A7 Am7/D D7
D.S. al Fine
feel - ing this way Has some - thing to do with you! It's a
f
sf
mf

IT'S THE LITTLE THINGS IN TEXAS

Words and Music by
RICHARD RODGERS

Copyright © 1962 by Richard Rodgers
Copyright Renewed
WILLIAMSON MUSIC owner of publication and allied rights throughout the world
International Copyright Secured All Rights Reserved

Refrain
G(add9)
Gdim
D7
G(add9)
G
lit - tle things in Tex - as I love.
mp
Gmaj7
G
G(add9)
G
Gdim
D7
There's a girl with a ver - y small waist Who
G(add9)
G
A7sus
A7
G/D
gives me a ver - y small squeeze, But oh, her heart is big as
Am7
D7
Am7
D13
4fr
G(add9)
Gdim
Tex - as! It's the lit - tle things in

D7
G(add9)
G
Gmaj7
G
Tex - as I love.
When we
G(add9)
G
Gdim
D7
G(add9)
G
go for a ver - y small walk
Our talk is a ver - y small
A7sus
A7
G/D
D7
Fm/D
D7
G
talk
And some - how
we don't talk of
Tex - as.
G7
C
G
G7
C
This girl is full of grac - es,
She's cute in all the right
mf

G G7 C A7 D
plac - es, And who needs great big spac - es? Whee! I
G(add9) G Gdim D7
drew four ac - es! One lit - tle thing in Tex - as a -
G C G(add9) G Gdim D9 Am7/D D9
4fr
4fr
dores me, And it's the lit - tle things in Tex - as I
1
G A7 D7
love. It's the
2
G C G
love.
mp
f
sf

THE MAN I USED TO BE

Lyrics by OSCAR HAMMERSTEIN II
Music by RICHARD RODGERS

Copyright © 1955 by Richard Rodgers and Oscar Hammerstein II
Copyright Renewed
WILLIAMSON MUSIC owner of publication and allied rights throughout the world
International Copyright Secured All Rights Reserved

Refrain (light Schottisch tempo)
G Gmaj9 G6 Gmaj7
man I used to be, A hap - py man was he And
man I used to be, Would go to sleep at three Or
G C6 Am7 Cm
3fr
aim - less as a leaf in a gale. What - ev - er has be - come of that
four A. M. or sev - en or nine, And when his wea - ry head was - n't
Bm/D E+ E7 Am7 Am7/D G D7
light - heart - ed bum Who thought he had the world by the tail? The
near an - y bed, A ta - ble or a chair would be fine! A
G Gmaj9 G6 Gmaj7 G
man I used to be, His life was gay and free And aim - less as a cloud in the sky,
man with - out a goal, A sort of friend - ly soul, He liked to play the role of a host

C6 Am7 Cm Bm/D E+ E7
3fr
He thought he knew the game, Then a - long came a dame Who
To an - y thirst - y pal Or a cas - u - al gal Who'd
Am7 Am7/D G B
turned him in - to some oth - er guy. I've got am - bi - tion now, I've got a
stay to cook his cof - fee and toast. He was a ne'er do well Who would - n't
mf
Bmaj7 Emaj7 Em B
mis - sion, now I aim to reach the top of the tree. That oth - er
dare do well He nev - er saw the top of a tree. But kind of
G A13 Am7/D
5fr
fly by night Who flew so high by night, Has van - ished like a sail on the sea.
sad I was To see the cad I was Dis - solv - ing like a sail on the sea.

G Gmaj9 G6 Gmaj7

And I'll nev - er find that eas - y liv - ing, eas - y tak - ing, eas - y giv - ing
And I'll nev - er find that fa - tal - is - tic, free and eas - y e - go - tis - tic

p

G C6

fel - low that I used to call me, You can
op - ti - mist who used to be me, You can

A7 D7 1 G Em

nev - er find The man you used to be.
nev - er find The man you used to

mf

Am7 D7 2 G A7♭5 D7 G

The be.

sf

MORE THAN JUST A FRIEND

Words and Music by
RICHARD RODGERS

Copyright © 1962 by Richard Rodgers
Copyright Renewed
WILLIAMSON MUSIC owner of publication and allied rights throughout the world
International Copyright Secured All Rights Reserved

F
hog of mine.
Warm and
mp
C7
soft af - fec - tion lies
In your
F
teen - y ween - y eyes,
Sweet - hog of
C7
mine,
Sweet - hog of

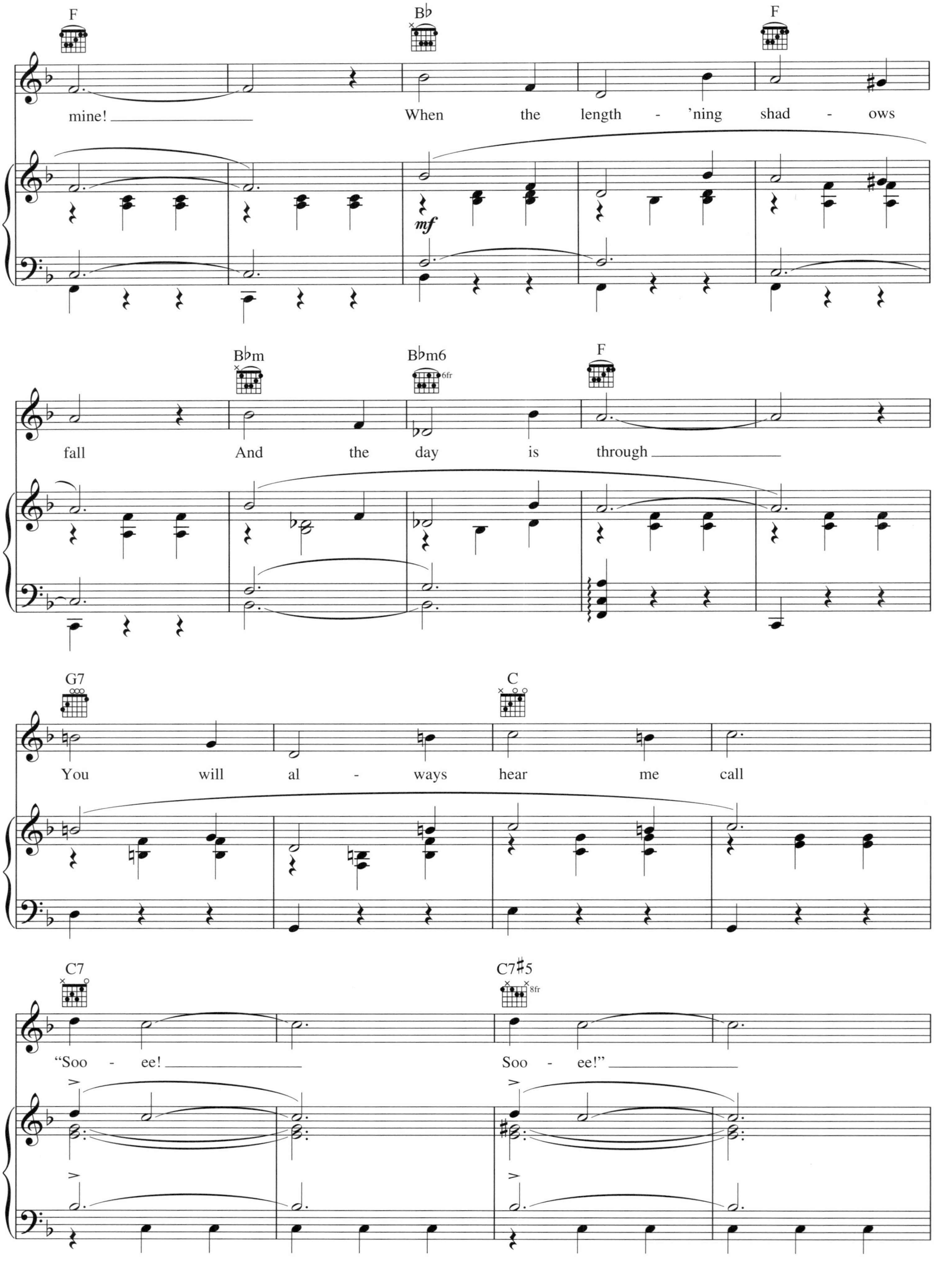
F
B♭
F
mine!
When the length - 'ning shad - ows
mf
B♭m
B♭m6
6fr
F
fall
And the day is through
G7
C
You will al - ways hear me call
C7
C7♯5
8fr
"Soo - ee!
Soo - ee!"

F
C7
Oth - er friends may drift a - way.
mp
F
Tell me that you'll al - ways stay,
C7
Gm
3fr
Sweet - hog of mine, (oink - oink) Sweet -
C7
1
F
B♭
F
C7
hog of mine!
f
2
F
mine!
8va
sf
Ped.
*

NEVER SAY "NO"

Words and Music by
RICHARD RODGERS

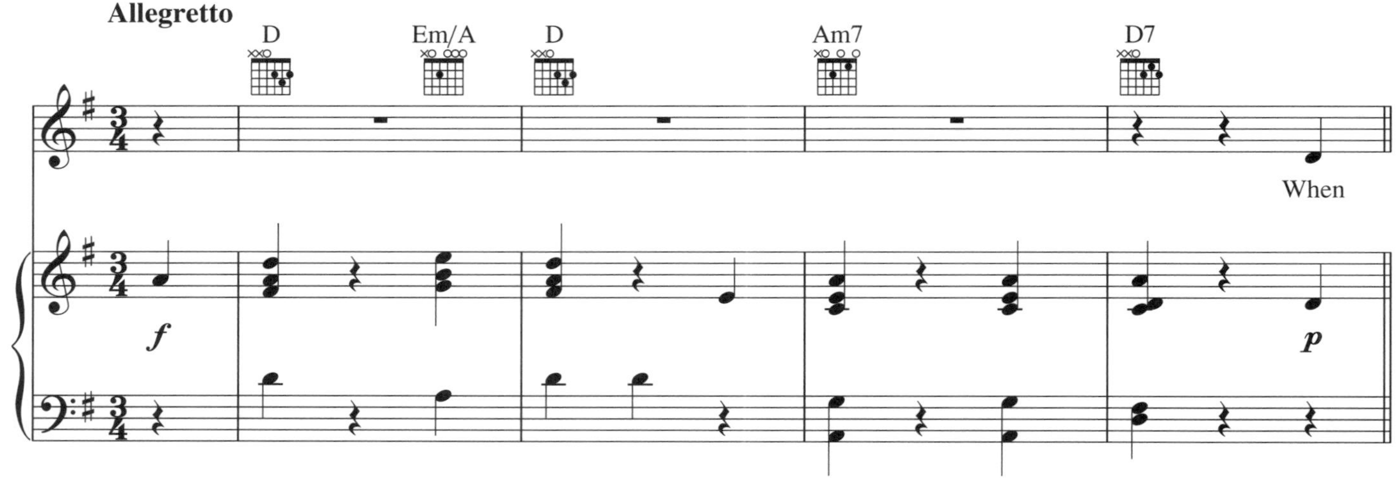

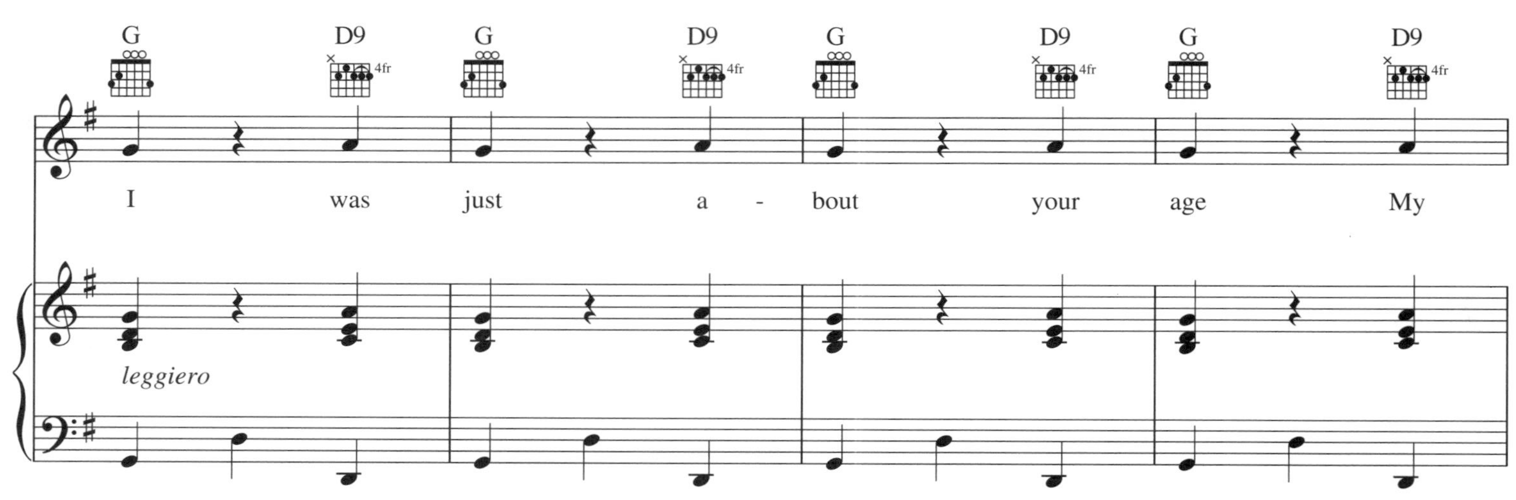

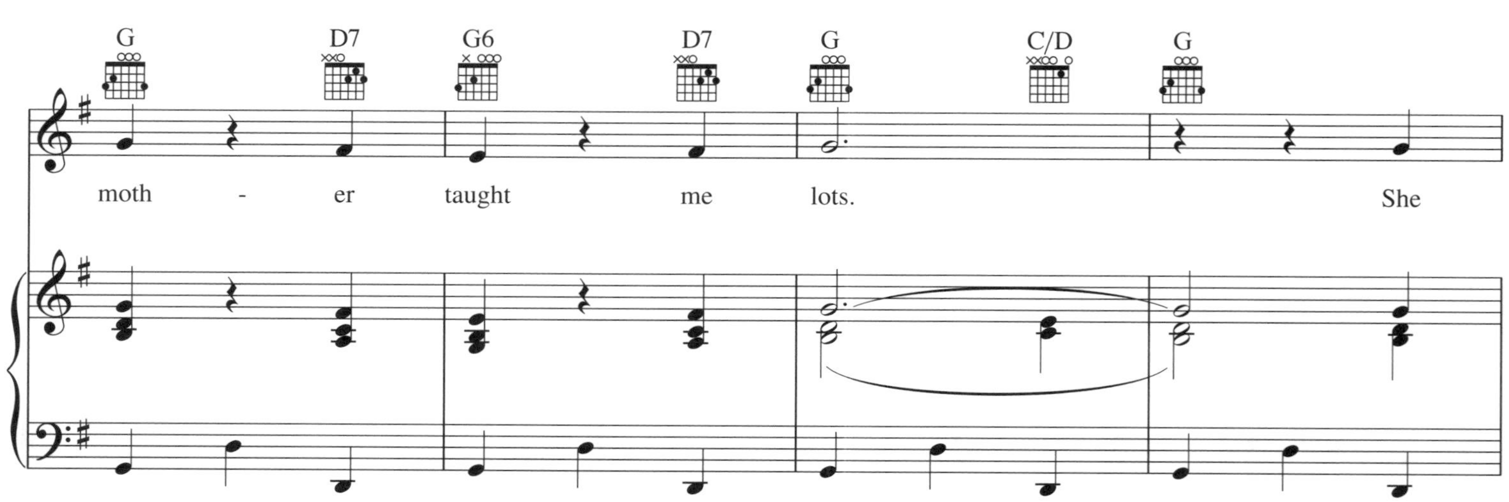

Copyright © 1962 by Richard Rodgers
Copyright Renewed
WILLIAMSON MUSIC owner of publication and allied rights throughout the world
International Copyright Secured All Rights Reserved

C
G9
9fr
C
G9
9fr
C
G9
9fr
C
G9
9fr
showed me how to clean a floor And
C
G7
C6
G7
C
F/G
C
B7/F♯
how to scour pots. She taught me
F7
E7
A7/E
E♭7
E♭7♯5
one thing more: A word that men ab -
Refrain
D7
G
D7
hor. Nev - er say "No" to a
mp

G
C/E
G/D
man.
Sim - ply a - void say - ing
C
Cm6
3fr
G/B
D7/A
"Yes" to him,
That leaves the ul - ti - mate
G
Gm6
3fr
D
A7
guess to him.
Dar - ling, don't ev - er say
D
D7
G
D7
"No."
Men find the neg - a - tive

G
C/E
G/D
rough.
Give an af - firm - a - tive
C
Cm6
3fr
G/B
D7/A
grin to him.
You need - n't real - ly give
G
Gm6
3fr
D
A7
in to him.
Don't use the pos - i - tive
D
G
B7/F♯
"No!"
"No" is a mean mon - o - syl - la - ble
mf

Em G7/D C E7
fit for a horse, A dog or a cow or a
Am/C Cm 3fr D7 D7♯5
calf. A nod or a smile would
G C/E A7/E A7♭5/E♭
cut the di - vorce sta - tis - tics by just a - bout
D7 G D7
half. "May - be," "Per - haps," "If I
mf

G
C/E
G/D
can," ___
These are some words that will
C
Cm6
3fr
G/B
D7/A
do as well. ___
Dar - ling, he's sure to love
G
Gm6
3fr
Am7
D13
4fr
you as well. ___
Nev - er say "No" to a
1
2
G
Em
Am
D7
G
D
G
man.
man. ___
f
f

THE NEXT TIME IT HAPPENS

Lyrics by OSCAR HAMMERSTEIN II
Music by RICHARD RODGERS

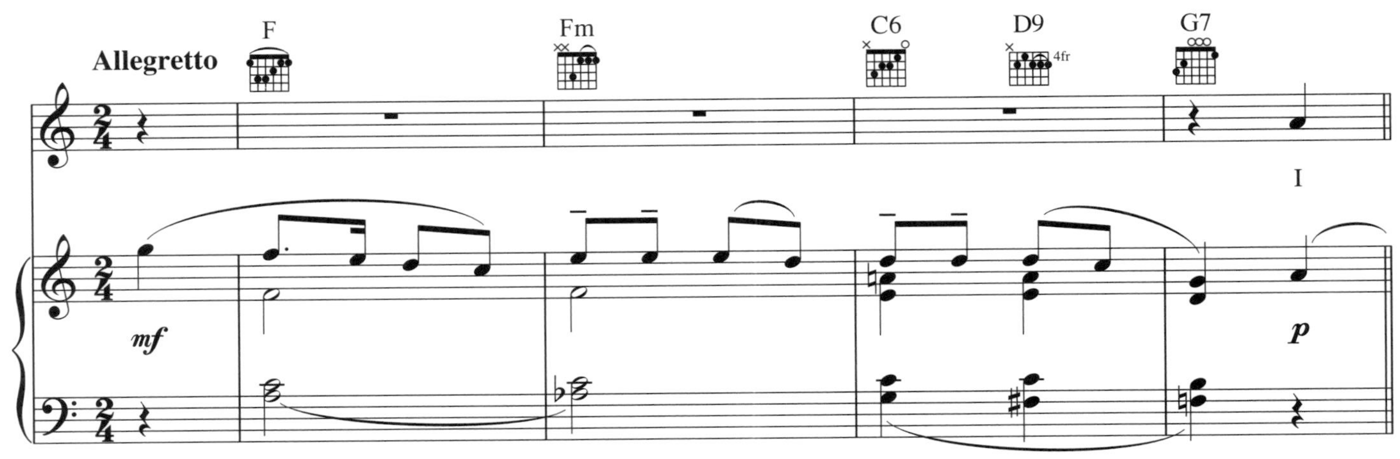

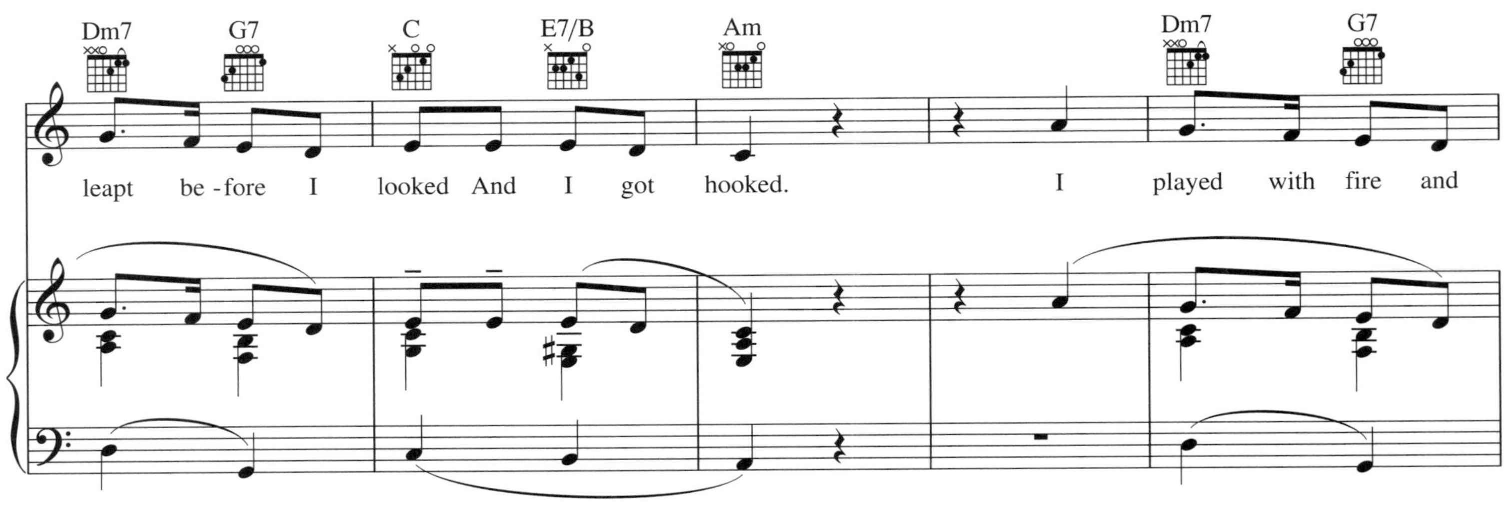

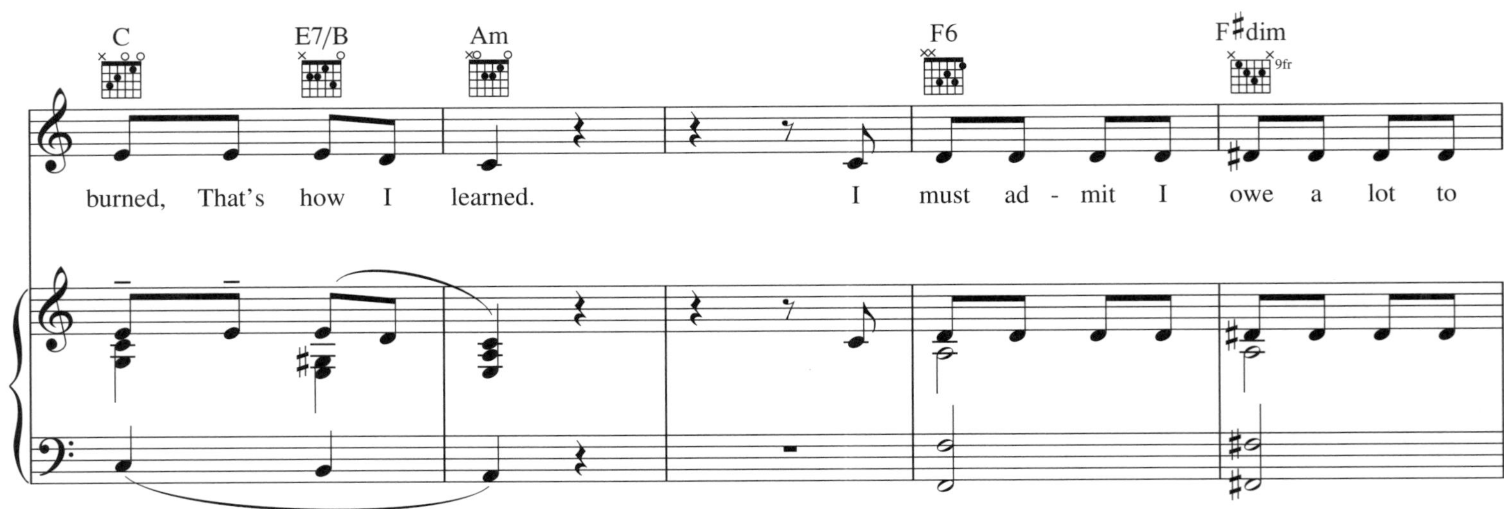

Copyright © 1955 by Richard Rodgers and Oscar Hammerstein II
Copyright Renewed
WILLIAMSON MUSIC owner of publication and allied rights throughout the world
International Copyright Secured All Rights Reserved

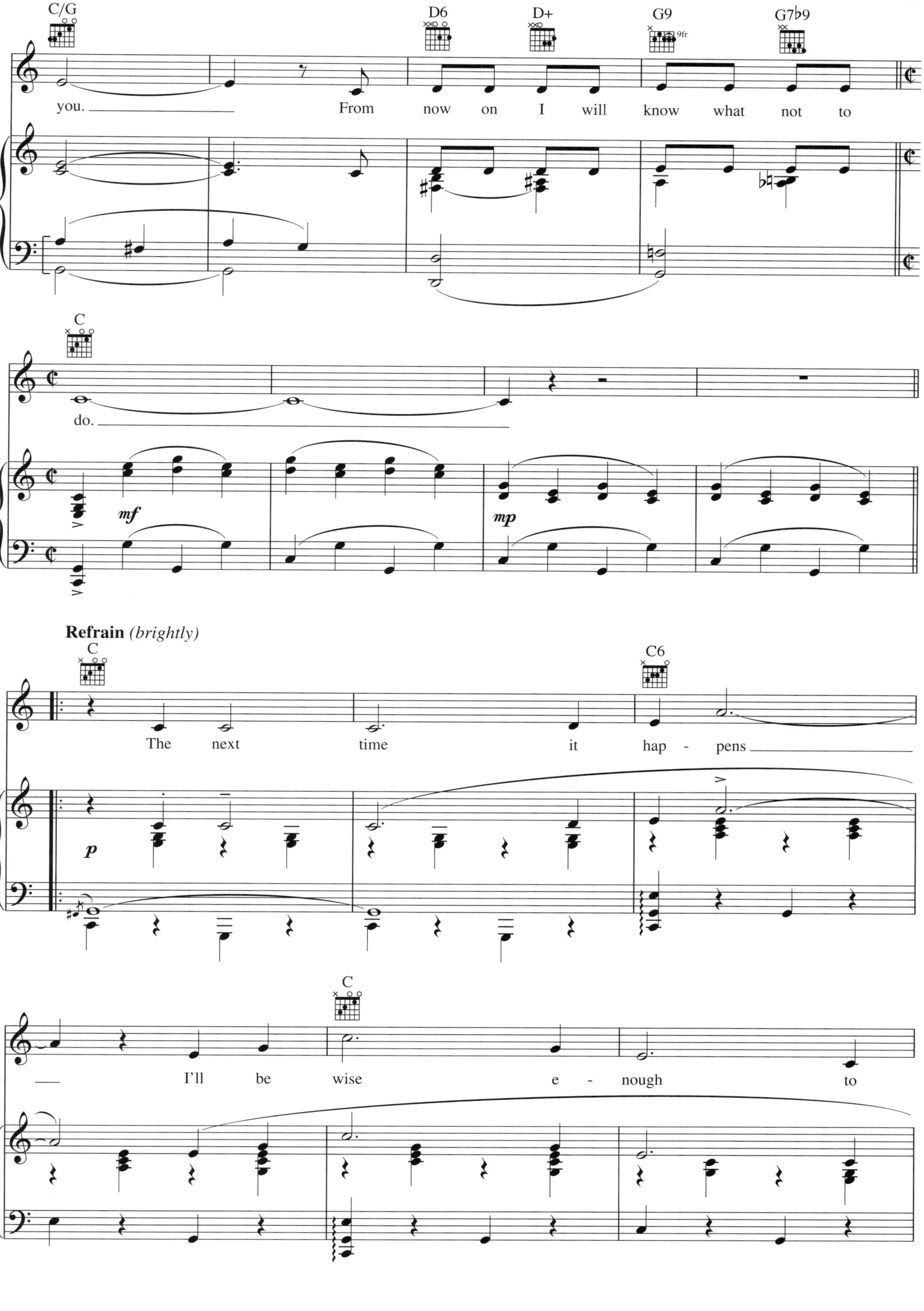
C/G
D6
D+
G9
9fr
G7♭9
you.
From now on I will know what not to
C
do.
mf
mp
Refrain (brightly)
C
C6
The next time it hap - pens
p
C
I'll be wise e - nough to

Dm7
G7
Dm7
G7
know
Not
to
Dm7
G7
Dm7
G7
Dm7
G7
Dm7
G7
trust
my
eye
-
sight
when
my
eyes
be
-
Dm7
G7
C
F
gin
to
glow.
The
next
time
B7
Cdim7
Em7
C
I'm
in
love
with

Dm7
G7
C+
C6
C
an - y - one like you,
My
G/D
Bm/D
G/D
G6/D
3fr
G/D
heart will sing no love song till I
cresc.
Am7
D7
G
know the words are true.
mf
G7
C
"The next time it
p

C6
C
hap - pens" What a fool - ish
thing to say!
Dm7
G7
Who ex - pects a mi - ra -
G9
9fr
cle to hap - pen ev - 'ry

C9
C7
F
day?
It
is
-
n't
B7
Cdim7
Em7
C
in
the
cards
As
Dm7
G7
C7
far
as
I
can
see
That
a
F6
C6
Dm7
C
thing
so
beau
-
ti
-
ful
and
won
-
der
-
cresc.

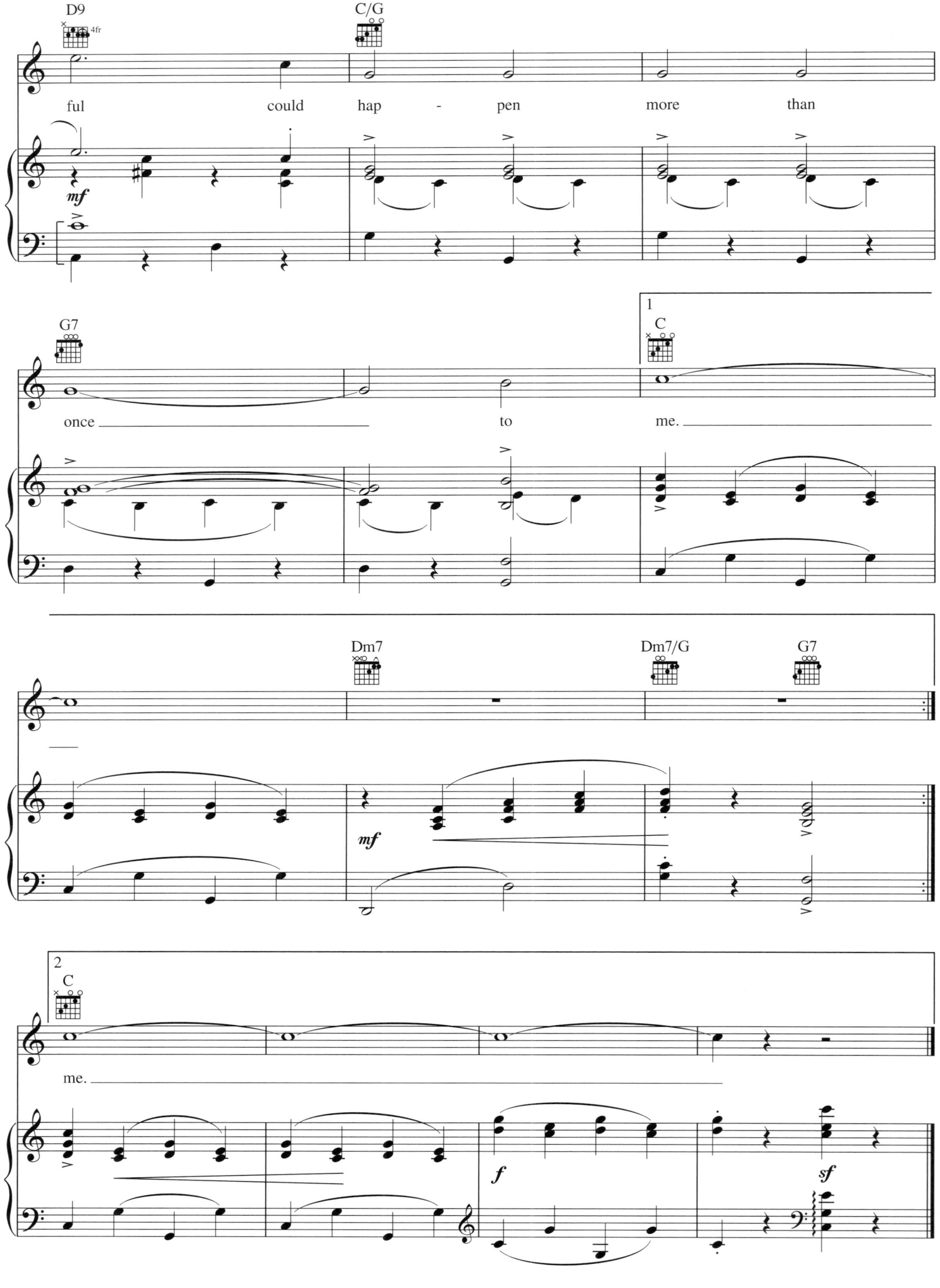
D9
4fr
C/G
ful could hap - pen more than
mf
G7
1
C
once to me.
Dm7
Dm7/G
G7
mf
2
C
me.
f
sf

SO FAR

Lyrics by OSCAR HAMMERSTEIN II
Music by RICHARD RODGERS

Copyright © 1947 by Richard Rodgers and Oscar Hammerstein II
Copyright Renewed
WILLIAMSON MUSIC owner of publication and allied rights throughout the world
International Copyright Secured All Rights Reserved

G9sus
G9
C
G9sus
G9
song that we love,
No scene to re -
C9sus
C7
F
Dm7
call
We have no tra - di - tions at
D7♭5/A♭
G7
Refrain (gracefully, not fast)
C
C6
all.
We have
poco rit.
p
G7
C
Am6/C
Cdim7
G7
noth - ing to re - mem - ber, so far,
so far,
So

C
Dm7
G7
C
far we have - n't walked by night and shared the light of a
Dm7
G9
9fr
C
C6
G7
star. So far your heart has nev - er flut - tered so
C
B7
Em
Am7
Am7♭5
G/D
E7
near, so near, That my own
Am
D7
Dm7
G7
heart a - lone could hear it, We

Gm7
C7
Gm7
C7
Fmaj7
F7
have - n't gone be - yond the ver - y be - gin - ning.
F6
F+
F
Em7
A7
Em7
A7
We've just be - gun to know how luck - y we
Dm
Dm7♭5
G7♭9
C
C6
are.
So we have
p
G7
C
C7
F6
Fm6
noth - ing to re - mem - ber, so far, so far, But
3
mf

C G7 C
now I'm face to face with you and now at last we've
marcato
Gm7 C7 E/F F E/F F Am7 Bm/A C/D D7
met, And now we can look for - ward to the
C E+ Fmaj7 G7 1 C Am7
things we'll nev - er for - get!
Dm7♭5 G7♭9 2 C C(add9)
get!
mf rit.
R.H.
Ped.

OUR STATE FAIR

Lyrics by OSCAR HAMMERSTEIN II
Music by RICHARD RODGERS

Copyright © 1962 by WILLIAMSON MUSIC
Copyright Renewed
International Copyright Secured All Rights Reserved

G G/B C6 D7 G G/B C D7 G G/B
our state fair is the best state fair in our state!
C D G G/B C D G G/B C6 D7
G G/B C6 D7 G G/B C D G G/B
state!
C D G G/B C6 D7 G

THAT'S FOR ME

Lyrics by OSCAR HAMMERSTEIN II
Music by RICHARD RODGERS

Copyright © 1945 by WILLIAMSON MUSIC
Copyright Renewed
International Copyright Secured All Rights Reserved

D7
G
Gdim7
Fate gave me no warn - ing.
G
D7
G
D7
Great was my sur - prise I saw you
Refrain (slowly, with expression)
G
Gmaj7
G6
G
D7
stand - ing in the sun and you were some - thing to see.
p
G
D7/F♯
G7/F
C/E
I know what I like and I liked what I saw, And I
poco a poco cresc.

G/D
E♭/D♭
Am7/C
D7
Gmaj7
G6
G/B
Am7
D7
said to my - self, "That's for me!" "A love - ly
mf
G
Gmaj7
G6
G
D7
morn - ing," I re - marked And you were quick to a - gree. You
p
G
D7/F♯
G7/F
C/E
G/D
E♭/D♭
want - ed to walk and I nod - ded my head as I breath - less - ly said,
Am7/C
D7
G
Cm7
3fr
Cm7/F
8fr
"That's for me!" I left you stand - ing un - der
mf
mf

F7 B♭ D7/A G D7/F♯

stars, The day's ad - ven - tures are through There's noth - ing for me but the

p

G7/F C/E G/D E♭/D♭ Am7/C D7

dream in my heart And the dream in my heart, That's for

mf

G7 Em/G G7 Fmaj7/G G7 Cmaj7 C Am9 D7

5fr

you! Oh, my dar - ling, That's for

1 G B♭dim7 D7/A D7

you! I saw you

mf

2 G Gmaj7 C/G G

you!

f

THAT'S THE WAY IT HAPPENS

Lyrics by OSCAR HAMMERSTEIN II
Music by RICHARD RODGERS

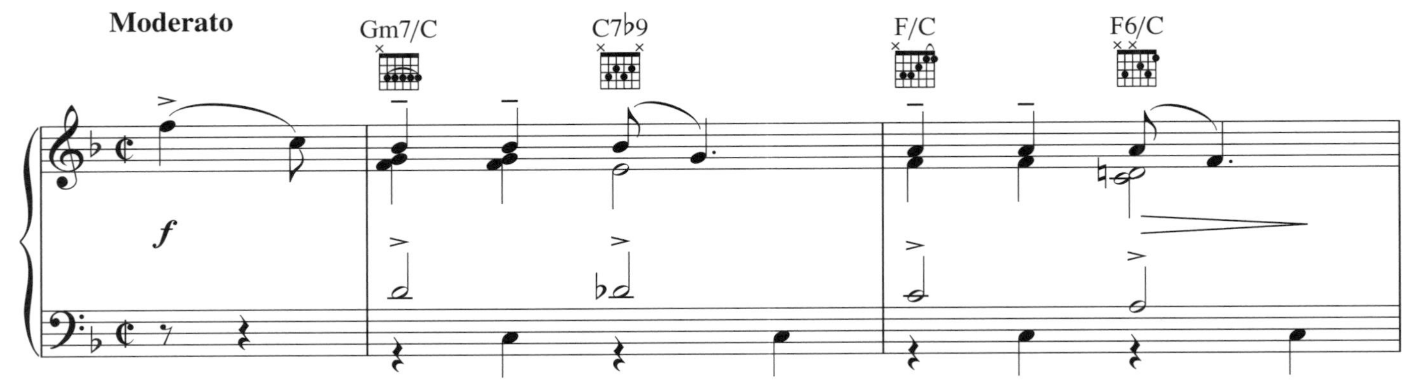

Copyright © 1953 by Richard Rodgers and Oscar Hammerstein II
Copyright Renewed
WILLIAMSON MUSIC owner of publication and allied rights throughout the world
International Copyright Secured All Rights Reserved

F F9 B♭6 Gm7♭5 F

wish you were a mile or so from Mich - i - gan Lake, __ Home with your moth - er and a

mf

B/C C7 F F/A B♭ F/A B♭m

T - bone steak. __

f *deciso*

F/C B/C C7 F Dm

Then a - long comes a fel - low with a

p

Gm7 C7 F Dm Am C7

smile like a kid, And he gets your at - ten - tion with a time - ly bid. __ He

F
F9
B♭6
Gm7♭5
F
says he knows a bis - tro where they give you a break, _ With french fried po - ta - toes and a
mf
B/C
C7
F
F/A
B♭
F/A
B♭m
T - bone steak. _
f
deciso
F/C
B/C
C7
F
Dm
You are shy and un - cer - tain, but he
p
Gm7
C9
F
Dm
Am
C7
pleads and you yield, And you don't have an ink - ling that you're signed and sealed, _ By

F
F9
B♭6
Gm7♭5
F
mere - ly tell - ing some - one you'd be glad to par - take
Of french fried po - ta - toes and a
mf
B/C
C7
F
B♭6
T - bone steak. That's the way it hap - pens,
That's the
mf
F
F+(♯4)
way it hap - pens,
That's the way it
cresc.
C9
F6
Gm7
Am7
B♭maj7
Am7
Gm7
Fmaj7
F
hap - pened to me.
f
8vb.

THIS ISN'T HEAVEN

Words and Music by
RICHARD RODGERS

Copyright © 1962 by Richard Rodgers
Copyright Renewed
WILLIAMSON MUSIC owner of publication and allied rights throughout the world
International Copyright Secured All Rights Reserved

Refrain (leisurely)
D
A7
D
This isn't heav - en, Who needs it? This is the earth and
mp legato
A9
5fr
A7
D
G♯m7
4fr
C♯7
you. You're not an an - gel, Who wants one?
F♯m
A9
5fr
D
You in the flesh will do. You're so real I'm
mf
Gmaj7
Gm6
3fr
D
Gm6
3fr
D
reel - ing. Who called you di - vine? Watch me walk a -

Bm7
E7
Em7
Em7/A
A13
5fr
cross the ceil - ing shout - ing, "You're mine! You're mine!"
D
G
F♯7
Bm
This is - n't heav - en, So what? You're not an an - gel,
mp
G
Gm
3fr
D/A
A9sus
A7
No you're not, You're mine, you're mine, you're
1
D
A7
mine!
f
2
D
G6
D
mine!
f

WHEN I GO OUT WALKING WITH MY BABY

Lyrics by OSCAR HAMMERSTEIN II
Music by RICHARD RODGERS

Quasi Cakewalk, in 2

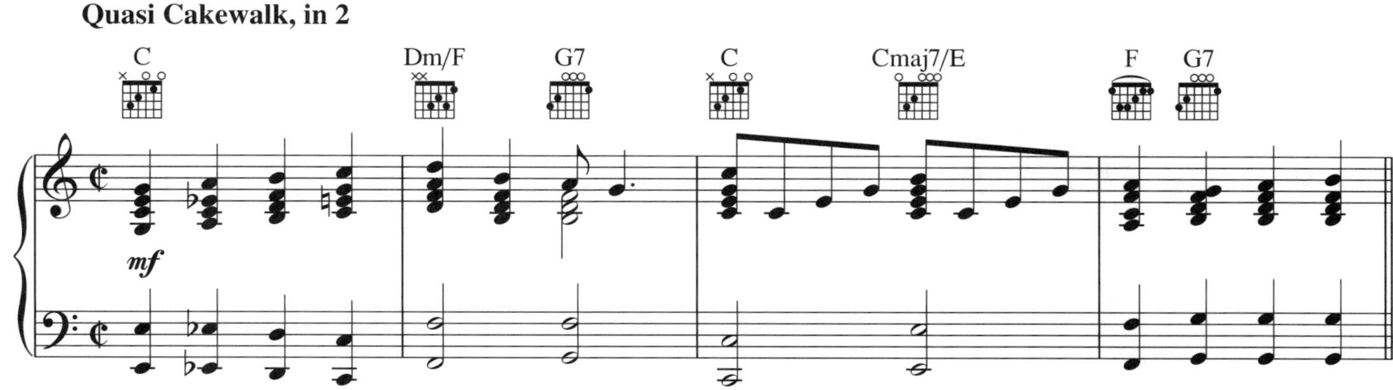

C
G7sus

When I go out walk - in' with my ba -

G7
C

by, stars are danc - in' in my ba - by's eyes!

Copyright © 1985 by The Estate of Richard Rodgers and The Estate of Oscar Hammerstein II
WILLIAMSON MUSIC owner of publication and allied rights throughout the world
International Copyright Secured All Rights Reserved

E♭dim7
G7/D
C
When I do the cake - walk with my
G
E7
A7
D7
ba - by, me and my ba - by al - ways win the
G7
C
prize! When I take her
G7sus
G7
home we start in spoon - in', spoon - in' suits my

E7
ba - by to a "T". Pret - ty
A7
D7
soon you're goin' to see some hon - ey - moon -
G7
in', 'cause if I don't mar - ry her, she'll mar - ry
C
1
B♭7♭9
Dm/A
G7
2
C
me!
me!

WILLING AND EAGER

Words and Music by
RICHARD RODGERS

Copyright © 1962 by Richard Rodgers
Copyright Renewed
WILLIAMSON MUSIC owner of publication and allied rights throughout the world
International Copyright Secured All Rights Reserved

Refrain *(Moderato con moto)*

E♭/B♭
6fr
D/B♭
6fr
Fm7/B♭
Here I am,
Look a-
mf
B♭7
D
E♭
3fr
D9
4fr
G7
round.
Will - ing and ea - ger and
mp
C7
F9
E♭/B♭
6fr
F♯dim7/B♭
Fm9/B♭
B♭9
hap - py to be
Half of you and
mf
1
E♭
3fr
B♭7
me.
2
E♭
3fr
me.
p
Ped.
*

YOU NEVER HAD IT SO GOOD

Lyrics by OSCAR HAMMERSTEIN II
Music by RICHARD RODGERS

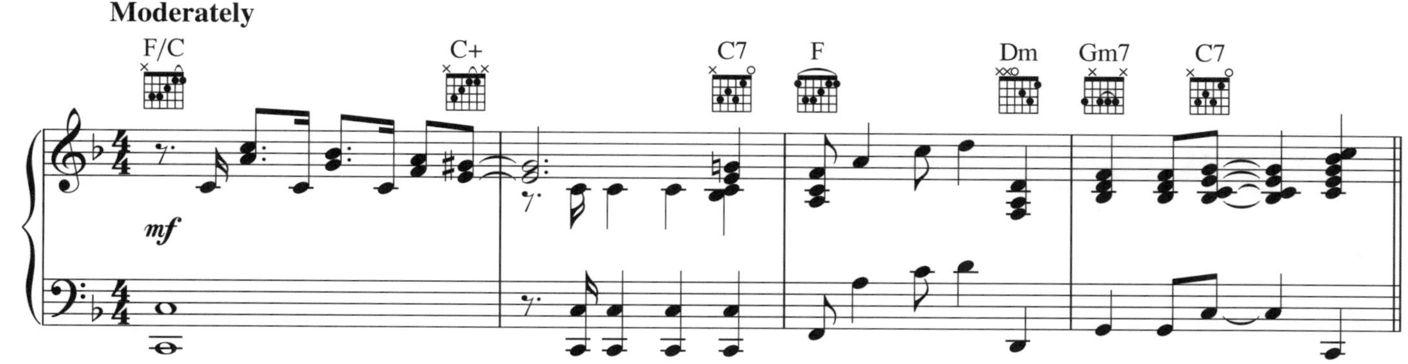

Copyright © 1985 by The Estate of Richard Rodgers and The Estate of Oscar Hammerstein II
WILLIAMSON MUSIC owner of publication and allied rights throughout the world
International Copyright Secured All Rights Reserved

F
C+
Gm/B♭
C
C+
F
You nev-er had it so good,
You cra-zy at-trac-tive mug, you!
Em7♭5
Gm/C
3fr
F
Gm/B♭
C7
F6
F
A♭dim7
Show your ba-by you're grate-ful
Or ba-by's go-ing to slug you.
I'll
C7
F6
C7
F
A♭dim7
sew, I'll bake.
I'll try to make your eve-nings all en-chant-ed.
My
C7
F6
G7
C7
N.C.
hon-ey cake,
I'm yours to take,
But don't take me for grant-ed!

F
C+
Gm/B♭
C
C+
F
Just do what an - y - one would; _
Con - fess you're a luck - y fel - ler.
Em7♭5
Gm/C
3fr
F
Em7♭5
A7
Come to ba - by and tell her
You've been mis - un - der - stood. _
D9
4fr
D7♯5
G13
3fr
G7
F/C
C+
C7
Kiss your ba - by and tell her
You nev - er had it so good, _ so
1
F
Dm
Gm7
C7
good.
2
F
Gm7
C7
F
good. _

RODGERS AND HAMMERSTEIN™
VOCAL SELECTIONS

ALLEGRO
HL00312007 . . . .$10.95
Come Home • A Fellow Needs a Girl • The Gentleman Is a Dope • Money Isn't Ev'rything • So Far • You Are Never Away

CAROUSEL
HL01121008 . . . .$10.95
If I Loved You • June Is Bustin' Out All Over • Mister Snow • A Real Nice Clambake • Soliloquy • What's the Use of Wond'rin' • When the Children Are Asleep • You'll Never Walk Alone

CINDERELLA
HL00312091 . . . .$10.95
Boys and Girls Like You and Me • Cinderella March • Cinderella Waltz • Do I Love You Because You're Beautiful? • Impossible • In My Own Little Corner • Loneliness of Evening • A Lovely Night • Stepsisters' Lament • Ten Minutes Ago

FLOWER DRUM SONG
HL00313225 . . . .$12.95
Chop Suey • Don't Marry Me • Fan Tan Fannie • Grant Avenue • A Hundred Million Miracles • I Am Going to Like It Here • I Enjoy Being a Girl • Love, Look Away • My Best Love • Sunday • You Are Beautiful

THE KING AND I
HL00312227 . . . .$14.95
Getting to Know You • Hello, Young Lovers • I Have Dreamed • I Whistle a Happy Tune • The March of the Siamese Children • My Lord and Master • A Puzzlement • Shall I Tell You What I Think • Shall We Dance? • Something Wonderful • We Kiss in a Shadow • Western People Funny

ME AND JULIET
HL00312256 . . . .$10.95
The Big Black Giant • I'm Your Girl • It's Me • Keep It Gay • Marriage Type Love • No Other Love • That's the Way It Happens • A Very Special Day

OKLAHOMA!
HL00312292 . . . .$14.95
All Er Nothin' • The Farmer and the Cowman • I Cain't Say No • Kansas City • Lonely Room • Many a New Day • Oh, What a Beautiful Mornin' • Oklahoma • Out of My Dreams • People Will Say We're in Love • Pore Jud • The Surrey with the Fringe on Top

PIPE DREAM
HL00312320 . . . .$10.95
All at Once You Love Her • All Kinds of People • Everybody's Got a Home But Me • The Man I Used to Be • The Next Time It Happens • Suzy Is a Good Thing • Sweet Thursday

THE SOUND OF MUSIC
HL00312392 . . . .$14.95
Climb Ev'ry Mountain • Do-Re-Mi • Edelweiss • I Have Confidence • The Lonely Goatherd • Maria • My Favorite Things • An Ordinary Couple • Sixteen Going On Seventeen • So Long, Farewell • Something Good • The Sound of Music • Wedding Processional

SOUTH PACIFIC
HL00312400 . . . .$14.95
Bali Ha'i • Bloody Mary • A Cock-Eyed Optimist • Dites-Moi (Tell Me Why) • Happy Talk • Honey Bun • I'm Gonna Wash That Man Right Outa My Hair • My Girl Back Home • Some Enchanted Evening • There Is Nothin' Like a Dame • This Nearly Was Mine • Twin Soliloquies (This Is How It Feels) • A Wonderful Guy • You've Got to Be Carefully Taught • Younger Than Springtime

STATE FAIR
HL00312403 . . . .$14.95
All I Owe Ioway • Boys and Girls Like You and Me • Isn't It Kinda Fun • It Might As Well Be Spring • It's a Grand Night for Singing • It's the Little Things in Texas • The Man I Used to Be • More Than Just a Friend • Never Say "No" • The Next Time It Happens • Our State Fair • So Far • That's for Me • That's the Way It Happens • This Isn't Heaven • When I Go Out Walking with My Baby • Willing and Eager • You Never Had It So Good

Prices, contents and availability subject to change without notice.

For More Information, See Your Local Music Dealer,
Or Write To:

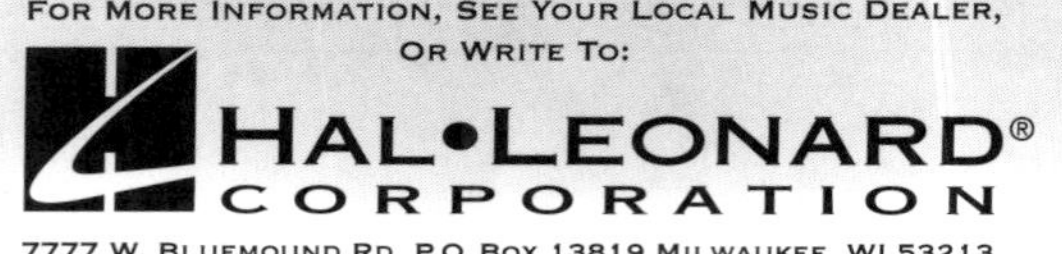

7777 W. Bluemound Rd. P.O. Box 13819 Milwaukee, WI 53213